Silica

The Forgotten Nutrient

Silica
The Forgotten Nutrient

Healthy skin,
Shiny hair,
Strong bones,
Beautiful nails

A guide to the vital role of
organic vegetal silica in nutrition,
health, longevity and medicine

by Klaus Kaufmann   Second Edition

With an introduction by Johannes Schneider MD
Foreword to the First Edition by Betty Kamen PhD

Published by Alive Books
PO Box 80055 Burnaby BC Canada V5H 3X1

Cover Photo: Clas Göran Carlsson
Back Cover Photo: Siegfried Gursche
Typesetting/Layout: Marian MacLean, Sheila Adams
Cover Design: Bill Stockmann

Printing, first edition - August 1990
Printing, second edition - September 1993

Canadian Cataloguing in Publication Data
Kaufmann, Klaus, 1942 -
  Silica: the forgotten nutrient

  Includes bibliographical references and index.
  ISBN 0-920470-25-4

  1. Silica-Metabolism. 2. Health. I. Title.
TX553.S5K38 1993   612.3'924   C93-091676-X

Printed and bound in Canada

Dedicated

to

Gabrielle

Acknowledgements

Many people have contributed to the effort of writing this book, and I offer my appreciation and thanks to them all. Uppermost in my mind is Siegfried Gursche, my publisher, who provided the opportunity and encouraged me along the way. Siegfried also kindly advanced me the funds to get the computer on which I began storing research material over a three-year period, and made available the extensive Alive Books library.

Hokan Cederberg provided expert scientific counsel and took the trouble to send copies of the original manuscript to silica researchers and scientists in places as far apart as Boston, USA, Paris, France and Forserum, Sweden for their review and comments.

Gisela Temmel edited the second edition. Gisela's command of the English language and her considerable talents as editor bestowed greater clarity and consistency throughout the work.

As always, my deepest gratitude goes to my wife, Gabrielle, who provided needed financial support, didn't object to the many nights I was closeted in my study, and patiently served as a sounding board for my ideas.

Contents

Foreword to the Second Edition   xiii

Foreword to the First Edition   xvii

Introduction   xxi

1. The Calcium Swindle   1

2. Meet the Flint Stones   5

3. Biological Transmutation   9

An Element of Higher Evolution   9

Humpty Dumpty's Enigma   12

Wherefrom the "Extra" Calcium?   15

Silicic Metamorphosis   16

Silica's Assimilation of Phosphorus   18

The Dance of the Elements   19

Amazing Silica Powers   21

Silica in Wonderland   21

A Question of Balance   23

4. Of Tall Horsetail Extraction   27

Well-Bred *Equisetum arvense*   27

Fairy Horsetails   28

Acquiring Horsetail Sense   28

A Polished Breed   29

Tracing the Elements   29

Horsetail Powerhealing   32

Of Aqueous Extraction   33

5.	**Picking a Bone With Calcium**	35
	No Life Without Silica	35
	Healing Animals	36
	Mineral Supermarket	36
	Ousting Osteoporosis	37
	The Dirty Dozen	39
	A Natural High	40
6.	**Nature's Internal Cosmetic**	43
	Beauty More Than Skin-Deep	43
	Collagen and the Silica Connection	44
	Into the Last Stretch	47
	Racing Against Inflammation	47
	A Horsetail by Any Other Name	48
	Bouncy Skin	48
	Tough as Nails	49
	Hair That Glows	50
	Teeth and Gums	51
7.	**Silica and the Aging Riddle**	53
	Youthful Aging	53
	Food for Thought	54
	Hair Repair	55
	Young at Heart	57
	Lung Repair	58
	Silicic Muscles	59
	Getting Under Your Skin	59
	Menopause Free of Stress	60
	Youth Pills	60
	Reducing Radiation Risks	61

Immune System Alert   62
Goodbye to Aching Joints   63
Live to 100!   65

8. **The Transmuted Healer Within**   67
    Therapeutic Vegetal Silica   67
    Employing a Healing Agent   67
    Diabetes Beaten   69
    Arterial Disease in Retreat   70
    Immunity to Tuberculosis   71
    A World Without Cancer   72
    No Room for Rheumatism   74
    Avoiding or Alleviating Alzheimer's   74

9. **Why I Supplement With Organic Vegetal Silica**   77
    Practicing Prevention   77
    Silica Banking   78
    The Good, the Bad and the Right Silica   79

10. **Horsetail Cooking**   83
    The Galloping Gourmet   83
    Horse Without Tail   84
    Sauerkraut, EFA and Other Good Advice   85
    Quenching Your Thirst   86
    Leftovers   86

Endnotes   89

Bibliography   93

Index   95

Useful Addresses   101

Foreword to the Second Edition

By threatening to ban a product, a government can accidentally improve our appreciation of its safety. During 1991, Canada's Health Protection Branch (HPB), concerned about possibly harmful ingredients reportedly found in horsetail, was intent on banning horsetail products in Canada. The HPB's concern was partially prompted by information supplied by the US Department of Agriculture.

Dr. James A. Duke, Economic Botanist at the National Germplasm Resources Laboratory of the Department, quoting a Kingsbury reference on the horsetail herb, was alarmed about reported poisoning of livestock. Livestock ate wild-growing horsetail of uncertain species, causing non lethal symptoms of poisoning. Ill effects were ascribed at least partially to the presence of the enzyme thiaminase in the green horsetail plant.

The proposed ban prompted a scientific presentation to the federal government. Concerned horsetail experts and scientists from Canada, France, Sweden and the USA arrived in Ottawa. Dr. Edith Carlisle of UCLA and others presented evidence in defense of spring horsetail.

The evidence showed that organic vegetal silica, derived from spring horsetail *(E. arvense)* by a process of aqueous extraction, renders the extracted silica safe for human consumption. Temperatures in excess of 150 degrees Celsius are attained during the extraction process. The heat-sensitive enzyme thiaminase, these experts showed, is either completely altered or neutralized during the heating phase of the extraction process. An independent laboratory confirmed that, at temperatures of over 150 degrees Centigrade, not only thiaminase, but all enzymes are permanently inactivated.

The scientists made it clear that in any event thiaminase is not a problem for the human metabolism, and is not poisonous to humans even if it is consumed. Of course, humans do not like livestock consume the fresh, green plant. According to a statement by Dr. Ernst Schneider, thiaminase does survive drying of the horsetail plant unaltered. He also stated that the symptoms appearing in grazing animals are based strictly on the consumption of *Equisetum pallustre* and its alkaloid pallustrin. The ban was lifted.

Since first publication, *Silica – The Forgotten Nutrient* has inspired some new skin care and hair care products. The makers of Dr. Kervran's Original Spring Horsetail Aqueous Extract are in the process of launching a number of body and hair care products using horsetail-derived silica. The Imedeen Skin Care Program babies the entire body's skin and the Samson Hair Care Program does the same for your hair.

I am told that Imedeen Skin Care supplies silica-rich nutrients not just to the face – the entire body is treated. A one month regime of Imedeen tablets complements the externally applied Imedeen beauty creams. A day cream, a night cream, and a body lotion complete the inside and outside regime. This skin care system provides advanced nutrient delivery to the entire skin structure.

A topical hair conditioner with bee pollen extract, a protein plus Silica Shampoo, and complementary silica tablets for hair care from the inside make up the Samson Hair Care Program. Clinical studies on these new products are under way according to the US manufacturer, Scandinavian Natural Health & Beauty Products Inc.

Other new or renamed products on the North American market are Flora Manufacturing & Distributing Ltd.'s

VegeSil Vegetal Silica – Dr. Kervran's Original Aqueous Extract of Spring Horsetail capsules (formerly called organic vegetal silica). SISU has brought out Kervran's Original Equilica Aqueous Horsetail Extract of Spring Horsetail (*Equisetum arvense*) tablets.

The growing number of organic silica products will ensure that Kervran's aqueously extracted silica from spring horsetail will not remain the "forgotten nutrient" for much longer. New approaches and findings of science are helping. Kervran's biological transmutation, as expounded in this book, is finding new acceptance among scientists.

In an essay entitled "Energetic Medicine" featured in the August/September 1991 issue of the well-respected *Townsend Letter for Doctors*, Dr. Paul D. Harris writes, "Biology, however, disobeys the entropic laws by controlled small-step interactions which obey a quantum pattern." This statement, echoed many times over in the literature, is a direct confirmation of biological transmutation.

Regarding the cover of this book, I have received criticism about the "hype"of using a glowing health club style beauty. Look at the front cover photo of Miss Universe, Yvonne Ryding. Is she not beautiful? There is something that the reviewer probably did not know: Miss Ryding is on record ascribing her glowing health and beauty in part to long term supplementation with Kervran's silica formula. She started a silica regimen in 1982. Two years later, in 1984, she was crowned Miss Universe. Yvonne Ryding is living proof that silica can beautify hair, skin and teeth. In my view, appearance is a mirror of how you take care of your body.

Klaus Kaufmann

Foreword to the First Edition

We are all naturally skeptical of a book that claims that a single nutrient can help cure everything from rheumatism to hair loss, facial wrinkles to osteoporosis. We may become even more skeptical when we learn that this nutrient – silica – is the second most abundant element on earth (second only to oxygen). Silica is as plentiful as sand on the beach – literally! Yet this substance has enormous capacity to turn the degenerative processes of aging and disease into the regenerative processes of healing and vitality.

Such skepticism is called for. Modern nutrition literature is a veritable jungle of conflicting theories, claims and special interests. Many advocates of various nutritional theories promote their particular regimen with all but religious fervor. *Silica – The Forgotten Nutrient* takes a more balanced approach. While the author presents a very broad and impressive body of knowledge about silica in this refreshingly short and concise work, he never loses the importance of other nutrients from sight. Klaus Kaufmann convinces you that the value of silica is real.

How is it that this "forgotten nutrient" has received so little attention, even in the alternative nutritional literature? Why has a mineral of power and importance been ignored for so long? The answer must be related to the fact that silica is so universal in biological processes – and so common in our environment – that it is taken for granted. For this substance to be used properly, it must be ingested in organic flavonoid chelated form. Many of our diets may be seriously deficient in this particular form of silica. Despite the abundance of this nutrient, most of us probably do not get nearly enough silica, even from an otherwise healthful diet!

Silica plays its most conspicuous role in calcium metabolism. A mounting body of evidence points to organic vegetal silica as the key factor in the control of osteoporosis, the debilitating decalcification of bones that has reached epidemic proportions among our older population.

Kaufmann suggests that, besides the presence of silica itself in bone structure, and silica's role in helping calcium utilization, there is a more fundamental and remarkable process taking place in our bodies. He presents compelling evidence to support Dr. Kervran's theory that silica atoms *transmute, in combination with oxygen, into calcium.* If this sounds to you like the nutritional version of cold fusion, you are not alone. Kaufmann acknowledges that there is scant acceptance of this theory throughout the scientific community, and leaves it entirely up to the reader to evaluate and decide.

Understanding the process is not the priority of this book, and it should not be yours, either. The huge body of empirical evidence presented in favor of the remarkable curative and preventive powers of organic vegetal silica is very convincing.

A friend once tried to pull off one of my long, hard fingernails. She was in total disbelief that the nails were my own. No hairdresser has ever worked on my hair without some comment about both the thickness and quality of my "mop." A recent biographical sketch that appeared in a journal after an interview surprised me with a description of my "flawless" skin. So you can see that this book is especially gratifying to me personally as a long-time advocate of horsetail extract, one of my favorite high-power, all-purpose elixirs.

Betty Kamen, PhD

*"One perceives the fundamental essence
of life in the living,
Not in the inanimate,
In that which is changing,
Not in what is finished."*

Goethe

Introduction

I am pleased to provide the introduction to an excellent new book on the tremendous benefits of organic vegetal silica, a subject that has been close to my heart, and I found very important to human health. Information on the potential benefits of supplementing your diet with organic vegetal silica has been sadly neglected by the popular press, and except a few scientific texts, very little information was available. Finally, a refreshingly new and vital presentation of this important data can be found in the pages of this book.

A friend first made me aware of the awesome potential of Silica in 1987. Like many others, I was getting more alarmed by the increasing incidence of the crippling disease of osteoporosis in the general population, especially in postmenopausal women. Since calcium supplementation did not seem to provide the entire solution, I began my own research on this abundant, vital plant.

To make my findings more available to the public, I wrote an article in *alive – Canadian Journal of Health and Nutrition*. There was such a tremendous response from the readers that I was asked to provide additional information on this alternative therapeutic, which I did in the *Focus on Nutrition series*, entitled "Silica – A Vital Element for Good Health," published by Alive Books. Unfortunately, earlier commitments made it impossible for me to pursue more detailed research on the nutritional significance of vegetal silica on bones, teeth, skin and hair. This is why I was doubly pleased to see that the author reviews the existing research, and is able to explain the essential value of this important nutrient in simple, easy-to-understand language. The reader benefits from the thorough review and straightforward manner in which the material is presented.

Klaus Kaufmann, with whom I have been acquainted for many years, has long been associated with the health food movement. He provides broad insight into the origins and uses of this deceptively simple and abundant plant, and how it gives us a key to vibrant good health. The medicinal properties of organic vegetal silica were first documented by a French scientist named Dr. Kervran, a man whose fascinating history is also presented in the book, along with a journey to the beginning of time, when giant horsetail plants provided nourishment for the prehistoric life forms of the day. I was entirely mesmerized and intrigued by the fascinating and in-depth treatment of silica that the author provides.

For readers from all walks of life looking for information on which to make intelligent decisions about their health, I take great pleasure in recommending the book.

Johannes Schneider, MD

1

The Calcium Swindle

Prescribing drugs to suppress symptoms is a standard medical approach to the treatment of disease. It seems that we have forgotten the root causes of illness. You have a headache – take an aspirin. You suffer from a calcium imbalance – take calcium. Isn't it too simple? Did you know that your doctor doesn't know why aspirin cures headaches, only that it does? Go ahead, ask your doctor. I'm asking if doctors know that mineral calcium supplementation doesn't necessarily heal symptoms of calcium depletion, such as osteoporosis, or make up for the lack of calcium in the body.

Orthodox medicine argues that when bone calcium is vanishing from the bones, supplementing with mineral calcium can replace the depleted calcium. This belief is so widespread that calcium is added to many refined foods. Yet no amount of calcium can restore bones gone brittle. Calcium treatment neither effects a cure nor offers relief from discomfort. Brittle bones, decaying teeth and other degenerating support structures of the body go right on deteriorating. Often the afflicted person's condition worsens. They just won't respond to calcium therapy.

Unsuspecting women, anxious to protect themselves against the threatening and crippling disease of osteoporosis are particularly vulnerable to the calcium fraud that is being committed. Increasingly they are augmenting their diet with large quantities of calcium. Yet this is a perilous attempt to preserve or replace the bone calcium they are afraid of losing to degenerative disease and aging. People don't seem to realize that ingestion of mineral calcium could be downright dangerous.

There is a growing body of evidence that suggests that, instead of effecting healing, supplemental mineral calcium, on the contrary, accelerates the leaching away of bone calcium and by that hastens the degenerative process of osteoporosis and similar degenerative diseases that affect the supportive and connective tissues in the human body. Misguided sufferers are in urgent need of help. It is high time to put a stop to ingestion of huge quantities of mineral calcium, high time to stop "stoning" innocent victims to death.

"Well then," you may ask, "how am I supposed to replace the lost calcium that is vanishing from my teeth and bones?" Instead of turning to doctors and hospitals for dreaded treatments or drastic surgery to escape pain and misery, an extremely harmless and beneficial remedy from nature's herb garden is available. It is called silica and is the focus of this book.

Vegetal silica, in its organic form, is a hitherto neglected but most vital nutrient. Have you ever wondered where the human fetus obtains the large amounts of calcium needed to create its skeleton? The growing baby creates calcium from silica. Silica is the element that gives us bouncing babies. Already in 1952, researcher Javillier of France considered silica one of "the twelve major elements in the composition of living organisms." He and other researchers confirmed that silicon is not a trace element in the human body, as had long been thought by orthodox medicine. Something tells me that silica is that ancient philosophers' stone* we were and are always searching for, the ultimate remedy that has the power to transform our aging years into golden years. Silica can maintain firm skin and prevent wrinkles. Tremendous forces that beneficially affect supportive and connective tissues have been identified in silica.

I will present evidence supporting the urgency of substituting silica for calcium. The facts speak for themselves. Silica is the "uncharacteristic" nutrient that promises to be the world's most effective medicine against degenerative disease. Where do you find this forgotten nutrient? Where you find any nutrient – in your food! It is going to be sheer delight to share with you the realization of silica's awesome constructive properties, its absolutely unique healing abilities, and its mind-boggling restorative powers. You want to stay fit, trim and young-looking, and grow to be a hundred – maybe more – live forever? Silica could be your elixir. If you don't necessarily want to reach one-hundred, don't you want to keep healthy and be physically fit at age seventy?

A survey publicized during Expo'86 in Vancouver, B.C. revealed the astounding fact that most people do not wish to reach one-hundred. Why, I wonder? Are they perhaps just afraid that old age will bestow suffering through physical incapacity and pain? Silica could stop the pain and even restore the body's self-repair processes. Instead of numbing the body with drugs, silica can remove the root causes of degenerative ailments, particularly osteoporosis

---

* A mythical stone or substance much sought after by alchemists, who believed it had the power to change metals into gold and to grant eternal youth.

– a crippling disease very much in today's news because of an increasingly aging population whose numbers are growing daily as the baby boomers are reaching middle age.

Longevity for all is just around the corner. In the western region of Finland, for instance, an area where the soil is very rich in silica in comparison with the silica-impoverished eastern region, a decrease in mortality due to cardiovascular disease has been noted. Our most precious organs, our eyes, particularly the iris and cornea, are very rich in silica, pointing to the possible toning effect silica could have on weakening eyesight.

Silica has the inherent power to turn the progress of disease into a regenerative process. It may well be the most memorable panacea ever. I will have much to say on that matter later. For now I would like to acquaint you with some of silica's dazzling accomplishments – historically speaking. It involves an exciting journey to the very dawn of time.

2

Meet the Flint Stones

The word silica derives from the Latin terms *silex* or *silicis*, which in English is flint. Flint stones, when impacted or struck, emit sparks that can set tinder on fire. Using the spark of flint stones, man no longer needed to carry the "sacred fire" into the caves. The sparking properties of flint gave mankind more freedom and crucial control over the environment. Flint stones bestowed great progress and the prosperity of controlled heat. Much later, with the discovery of wooden matches, flint stones were forgotten – for a long while.

Then a time came when evolving man searched for a perfect cover for the ventilation holes in his dwellings that would keep out rain and cold but let in the light. Perhaps accidentally, he discovered that flint, as silicates, made ideal window panes. Yes, the most common silicate, silicon dioxide (SiO_2) delivers the raw material for glass. Again flint provided for man's well-being and comfort – soon taken for granted.

Silica again came to the rescue in modern times when electricians looked for a suitable semiconductor that would control the flow of electric charges. They discovered that silicon exhibited excellent semiconductive properties. This remarkable capacity of flint revolutionized the electronics industry. North America decided to honor the ancient flint stones by naming a giant electronics district "Silicon Valley." Today people consider the personal computer to be the invention of the century, having the greatest impact on their lives (and most definitely on mine!). Thanks to the flint stones I can save weeks of work by committing this text to the memory chips of my computer.

There is more. Did you know that the flawless beauty of quartz, as exemplified by the purple amethyst is nothing less than – you guessed it – silicon? More correctly, it's silica. Silicon is one of the few elements (others are potassium and sodium) that cannot exist in isolation on earth. Only the interior of the sun can hold single silicon atoms. On this planet silicon is always joined to other atoms, creating useful compounds like silica crystals. And those siliceous crystals are swinging with the times; they even make modern clocks accurate with their "timely" vibrations.

While cheering silica, I might as well add that:
• Petrified wood owes its eternal life entirely to silicification, a natural process during which wood is impregnated with silica.
• Silicon carbide ranks high among the hardest minerals known, close in hardness to the coveted diamond.
• Industrial desiccated silica gel is a highly adsorbent (means condensing and holding upon a surface) colloidal, used to deodorize and clean air – yes, silica has deodorizing powers too – and more!*

* There is another kind of mineral–silica gel that is made from pure quartz crystals as a therapeutic gel. This, however, deserves a book by itself. I recommend reading the companion volume Silica–The Amazing Gel which reveals the secrets of therapeutic silica gel.

Not surprisingly, silicon is the most important element on earth after oxygen. Luckily it's also a most abundant element, making up 40 percent of earth's crust. More awesome, research has proven that silicic acid, a compound of silicon and water, was one building block of the primary substance from which life was created. The oxygen we breathe is derived up to 70 percent from ocean algae that are rich in silica content. The combined contribution from all other plant life makes up only 30 percent of the earth's oxygen mantle.

Modern science cannot answer all questions regarding the origins of life but in the last twenty years it has made tremendous progress in determining the essential ingredients that sustain and prolong life. Anti-oxidants that police and protect the organism have been discovered. One of the most important of these is silica.

The continued health of all organisms is dependent on organic vegetal silica, necessary for many metabolic functions. While no one nutrient can sustain all of man's complex organs, silica offers us the opportunity for increased well-being; a strong skeleton, sustained elasticity, and youthful vigor into our advanced years.

Why is organic vegetal silica so important in nutrition? How can it beautify? How can it keep us from getting old prematurely? Where can we find it and how can we assure sufficient intake of vegetal silica? These are vital questions that deserve investigation. Let us find out just why we must not ignore this indispensable nutrient any longer. We will begin by "transmuting" a questionable theory into general knowledge and conclude with useful information.

3
___

Biological Transmutation

An Element of Higher Evolution

I would like to familiarize you with perhaps the most remarkable, definitely the most questionable explanation first. In 1966, the French inventor, Professor Kervran, proposed a most astounding theory![2] Even today, although much discussed, it is still considered unscientific in orthodox science. However, because it addresses the biological function of vegetal silica, I am including it here on an anecdotal level.

In his controversial book *Biological Transmutations*, Kervran purports to show just how silica may work. Some things are known before knowing seems possible. For instance, newly born goslings swim right after they pick their way through the eggshell – there is no apparent learning process involved. No one taught the little geese. It's baffling but such wonders just cannot be explained because . . . well, some things just cannot be explained. This type of knowledge scientists call *a priori*.

The French scientist and lecturer, Professor Kervran, declared biological transmutation to be *a priori* knowledge.

He said, "incomprehensible as it seems, there nevertheless is in nature a constant movement from certain biological elements into other life elements." This theory is not fully appreciated by the classical sciences of chemistry and biology, although biological transmutation has been observed and such observation confirmed.

To understand scientific reluctance to accept this extraordinary explanation, we must go back to the 18th century to the French scholar Antoine Laurent Lavoisier. He had just laid the foundations for a chemical law that claimed the conservation of matter under all conditions. Lavoisier said that "nothing creates itself, in every operation, or reaction, there is an equal quantity of matter before and after . . . there is only exchange or modification."

In other words, he says that nothing is lost and nothing is created. Instead, every thing can undergo transformation and become a different thing. We can say that the law of conservation of matter states that the integrity or existence of an individual elementary atom, say a silicon atom, is always *preserved*. If it disappears at one point, it must reappear at another point.

A silicon atom cannot, according to Lavoisier, change into, let's say a calcium atom. This scientific law was, of course, perfect for his time. It seemed unshakable, remained undisputed for a hundred years, and is still widely accepted today – despite glaring conflict that emerged with the Twentieth century.

Humanity entered the *atomic age* and discovered that some elements can transmute into pure energy and are no longer matter at all. Matter is not preserved! Science discovered that matter can turn into pure energy through spontaneous nuclear disintegration, a natural process. This conversion we call *radioactivity*. But do elements transmute only through radiant energy? What does that have to do with silica? Let's backtrack a little to make this clearer.

Over 100 years ago, in 1878, the celebrated French biologist, chemist, and bacteriologist, Louis Pasteur prophesied a great future for silica as the nutritionally optimal therapeutic agent. He lived from 1822 to 1895. In his time he eased the toil of humanity. Pasteur set the stage for a new, gentle, natural method of preserving food. To this day this method is called pasteurization,* after its eminent progenitor.

Pasteur said that silicic acid, a compound of silica and water, is "called upon to play an important role in therapeutics." His prediction is being fulfilled in our time thanks to the discoveries of his compatriot, Professor Kervran – Nobel Prize nominee, scientist and researcher, member of the New York Academy of Science, and of the International Centre of Biological Research of Geneva, also a Director of the University of Paris.**

Professor Kervran was a true visionary in the spirit of his great forebear. Though still scientifically unprovable *in vitro*, his theories hold the greatest promise for the future.

Science has endeavored to explain radioactive transmutation of matter by applying to it Albert Einstein's theory of relativity. With the now world-famous formula $E=mc^2$, Einstein showed mathematically that at the velocity of light (c), energy (E) is equal to mass (m). The full impact of Einstein's formula became visible with the atomic bomb exploding over Hiroshima in 1945. It ushered in the

---

* A process which renders dairy products, wine and beer free of disease-producing bacteria and helps to prevent them from spoiling without destroying the vitamins or changing the taste.
** In 1983, while this book was still being formulated in my mind, Professor Kervan died.

11

atomic age. But until Kervran came along, Einstein's theories had never been studied from the biological viewpoint.

Because of variances in the theoretical law of the conservation of mass and energy, science couldn't explain fully just how biological transmutation occurs. Professor Kervran not only pointed out that biological transmutation exists, but he implied that it affects every phase of our lives. By change we create life, and life, Professor Kervran reasoned, does not fall within the limitations set by Einsteinian physics. The study of the continuous transmutational life processes *in vivo*, i.e., in the living body, was something more than could be explained by biology, physics or chemistry. A new name had to be coined for the scientific search into the mystery of life.

Humpty Dumpty's Enigma

The puzzle represented by biological transmutation is poignantly illustrated by Professor Kervran. In his book he tells of his childhood in Brittany. He grew up in an area full of slate and granite, rock composed of quartz, feldspar, and mica, but absolutely without limestone, a rock composed of calcium carbonate. His parents kept chickens that never received any limestone, nor was their diet in any way supplemented with limestone. Yet every day during the egg-laying season those chickens laid eggs with calcareous shells. Young Kervran observed that the chickens were incessantly scratching for fragments of mica that were strewn around the yard. The boy knew that mica, with feldspar and quartz, contains silica. Why did those chickens search for mica? He watched his mother open the gizzards of slaughtered chickens, finding small grains of sand, but never any mica. What had happened to the mica? How did the calcium get into the eggshell in an area lacking calcium?

This riddle intrigued Kervran all his life. Because no one could give him the answer, he decided to dedicate himself to the solving of this perplexing mystery. In so doing, he became a great discoverer and eminent scientist. He began his search in 1935 and along life's path learned of other secrets. One of them was very closely related to his boyhood discovery.

In 1822 the British scientist William Prout made a systematic comparative study of the amounts of calcium present in chicken eggs and the chickens hatched from them. To his bewilderment Prout found that the newly born baby chick contained four times more calcium than there was in the egg. Where did the extra calcium come from? He speculated that there was an unknown element that could transmute into calcium, but he never proved it. Without knowledge of transmutation, other scientists could not explain the phenomenon either. The calcium in the eggshell was still intact and, in any event, no calcium could cross through the embryonic membrane separating the chicken from the eggshell.

Simultaneously in Germany, a researcher, Vogel, found more sulphur in the sprouts of watercress he was studying, than were present in the seeds grown in distilled water only. He concluded from this discrepancy that sulphur could not be a "simple element." (He was wrong. Sulphur is an element.) But where did the extra sulphur come from?

Shortly after that, around 1870, researchers Rothamsted, Lawes and Gilbert found that plants could abstract more magnesium from the soil than it contained – more puzzles. In his professional capacity, Professor Kervran kept coming across ever more unexplained phenomena, similar in nature to the mysterious apparent calcium creation in the shells of chicken eggs and in baby chicks. He also found the same calcium inconsistencies in reptilian eggs.

Being an official of the French government, Kervran became involved in an investigation into the apparent poisoning deaths of welders. The victims all had come too close to the gas flames of their torches during the welding process. Kervran came to the conclusion that the welders' fatal accidents were due to carbon monoxide poisoning. However, only oxygen and nitrogen could be detected in the surrounding air. Despite this unexplained mystery, Kervran subsequently saved other welders' lives by introducing new safety regulations in the workplace.

Obviously lacking scientific proof, how could he deduce the presence of carbon monoxide, and where did this poison gas come from? Well, Professor Kervran remembered some similar incidents from his high school days. The classroom in which he studied was heated by a rustic cast iron stove that was apparently improperly insulated. Students constantly got headaches. Their teacher explained that this was due to carbon monoxide poisoning. At the time, Kervran had no reason to doubt this.

The true explanation came to him indirectly when he was already over 50 years old. It turned out that the nitrogen was responsible for producing carbon monoxide inside the body of the victims through biological transmutation. Replacing nitrogen with helium prevented further transmutational poisoning. Happily, Kervran was in a position of authority that permitted him to instruct factory inspectors accordingly. Further carbon monoxide poisonings, also known as oxycarbonic intoxication, could completely be avoided after that.

Still intrigued with the phenomenon of spontaneous change observed in the nuclear structure of elements,

Kervran turned his attention to the transmutation of sodium into potassium. In experiments he undertook in the Sahara desert with the assistance of the French military, he found confirmation of this transmutation taking place in the body. It is not within the scope of this present volume to detail his research into sodium-potassium transmutation. To interested readers I recommend Kervran's own text, *The Sodium-Potassium Bond*.

Humpty Dumpty's enigma that had puzzled Prout was eventually explained. Researcher Charnot found that the membrane that separates the egg from the eggshell contains silica. For 100 g of membrane, there are 154.79 mg of silica (SiO_2) in the inner leaf and 464.80 mg of silica in the outer leaf.

Wherefrom the "Extra" Calcium?

In 1959 Professor Kervran tackled the problem of explaining the biological transmutation of silica into calcium. During his research he noted that siliceous stone used in sculptures deteriorates over time and gypsum or carbonate of lime is formed instead, which ultimately disintegrates. This, incidentally, is the reason such monuments are periodically in need of restoration. Siliceous rocks can become calcareous through the agency of microorganisms.

Based on his study of ion exchange and his many other observations, Kervran assumed that biological transmutations of weak catalyzed energy take place in living organisms. With the assistance of enzymes they can transmute ions of one element into ions of another element and can even literally "melt" these ions to form new ions. In the same way, Kervran concludes, calcium could result from the fusion of:

1 ion Mg(magnesium) (=24) + 1 ion O(oxygen) (=16) or:
2 ions C(carbon) (=12x2) + 1 ion O(oxygen) (=16) or:
1 ion C(carbon) (=12) + 1 ion Si(silicon) (=28)

In other words, according to Kervran, both magnesium and silica are both principal sources of calcium in the human body! Expressed differently, it could be said that silica is an organic replica of calcium and silicon. Kervran's astounding hypothesis does explain some well-documented observations, most importantly:

1. The recalcifying action of silica in growth and in tuberculosis cases.
2. The human body can excrete more calcium than it receives, the extra calcium coming mainly from magnesium ions.
3. The calcification of atheroma: "calcium deposits itself when silica diminishes, as though a calcium-silicon balance were a normal metabolic condition" – the transformation of silicon and calcium explains the noted increase in calcium.

Before considering the professor's conclusions, let us take a closer look at the various interactions of which silica is obviously capable in living tissue.

Silicic Metamorphosis

Professor Kervran says that, in living bodies, silicon changes to calcium according to this formula:

14 silicon atoms plus 6 carbon atoms create 20 calcium atoms.

He points to the examples of the earthworms and microorganisms known as streptomyces that transmute silica into calcium. Many researchers have noticed that in certain demineralization, for example in the bone of the sufferer of tuberculosis or rachitis, the losses in calcium and in silica run parallel, though the loss of silica is always earlier and proportionally more important than that of calcium and the other minerals. What's more, in special ailments such as softening of the bones (osteomalacia), silica is almost totally absent in the bones, which are instead enriched with calcium fluoride, and magnesium. The credit for having recognized these curious migrations of calcium and silica goes to silica researcher A. Charnot. Others use silica to prepare for recalcification; researchers Renon, Lecler, and Chevalier prescribe silica as an aid in fixating calcium in the tuberculosis sufferer.

Rheumatologists also attach great importance to the silica-calcium balance. Professor Luithler considers silica a structural element on which the elasticity of tissue depends. When silica diminishes, calcium increases and elasticity suffers. This points to a preventive and alleviating influence of silica for sufferers of arthritis* as well.

What's the conclusion? At this point it seems appropriate to offer apologies to all those who have been taking calcium supplementation for stronger bones. The question arises: wouldn't they have been better off to supplement with vegetal silica instead? Seemingly – yet – there is no doubt that calcium reinforces vitality and endurance inside the body. It also buffers the all-important acid-alkaline equilibrium efficiently.

If there were an excess of calcium in the bloodstream, calcium crystals would be amassed in all the soft tissues throughout the body. Inevitably they would sabotage vital organs and arteries. Therefore, perhaps calcium supplementation is not the answer to protecting your bones. On the other hand, a continued lack of calcium over a long period would lead to tetany, a disease of the diaphragm and heart muscle that causes death. To supplement with calcium or not to supplement – that is the question. But

* If you suffer from arthritis you should check your acid-alkaline balance. If it is impaired, a juice fast could further positively influence the acid-alkaline balance. You can find out how to prepare for a juice fast by reading my book *The Joy of Juice Fasting*.

need we worry? After all it turns out that the human body prudently maintains calcium in balance, protecting life. Yes, you say, but what about protecting the bones? Well, it seems that transmutation of silica, if proven also *in vitro* (empirical or *in vivo* evidence is presented throughout this volume and emphasized in the second volume *Silica – The Amazing Gel)*. could be the answer to both problems because the problems arising from bone calcification are intimately connected to and coincide with a decrease in the quantities of silica.

Still (though empirical data does not support this) researchers Charnot and Kervran agree that caution in supplementation must be exercised, that "supplementation of mineral silica in the daily required amount cannot transmute into calcium because:

• The supplementation of mineral silica causes the transfer of calcium from the bones to other tissues.
• But organic vegetal silica, contrary to mineral silica, transfers calcium to the bones!"

Charnot cured a patient of deforming and joint-stiffening rheumatism through the administration of organic silica.[11] This is excellent news for sufferers of bone disease.

Silica's Assimilation of Phosphorus
Meanwhile, two researchers, Berthelot and Andre,[12] described the biological interdependence of silica and phosphorus and how silica promotes assimilation of phosphorus. Phosphorus tissues easily retain silica so that one can find silica in the phosphorus-rich brain tissue. It follows that when phosphorus therapy or supplementation is prescribed, simultaneous supplementary silica therapy should be considered. Not surprisingly, both silica and phosphorus are of special significance in the treatment of many nervous disorders. They are also helpful in the relief of asthenia, a debilitating body weakness.

Silica researcher Charnot, noted in his observations on the problems of calcification in some ailments occurring in horses, could "reattach" silica to the random migrations of calcium and phosphorus that the amounts of silica diminished in all the following body functions and organs: in bile, the adrenal, cartilage, teeth, muscles, nails, skin, hair, lungs, spleen and blood. In the teeth and bones, which normally are important reserves of silica and calcium, all traces of silica tended to vanish completely.

On the other hand, nerve tissues like the brain, cerebellum and marrow, rich in phosphorus, registered an increase in silica.[13]

His experiments show that all problems in the metabolism of calcium can be said to be caused by decalcification (as in tuberculosis) or by hyper-calcification of the bone. This led to the conclusion that calcium migrations seem to provoke an exaggerated consumption of body silica, while the storage of body silica in the nervous tissue suggests two possible reasons:

a) The organism, while recuperating, during the reorganization of its silica, stores it in phosphor-rich tissues because they are best suited to contain it. Silica scientists Berthelot and Andre[14] have already shown the interdependence of silica and phosphorus, and how silica "prefers" the assimilation of phosphorus.

b) A substitution for silica or phosphorus has formed in the presence of an excess of circulating silica.[15] Perhaps not surprisingly, two other researchers, Hall and Morisson, have proven that silica can replace phosphates.

The Dance of the Elements

We are referred back to the chicken theory. Kervran conducted some research to confirm the bond between calcium, potassium and magnesium. To prove transmutation of potassium to calcium, he put some hens into a chicken run and left them without access to lime. As expected, after some days they had used all their calcium reserve and laid soft-shelled eggs. That day they were given a supply of pure analyzed mica. The hens, controlled from birth, had never seen mica, but fell upon it with relish. The following day the eggs had normal shells. In this experiment the transmuted calcium came from potassium.

Sodium is very similar to potassium. Kervran concludes that potassium in the human body derives mainly from sodium. However, sodium is associated with several ailments, notably high blood pressure in which sodium intake might have to be reduced. Therefore, to combat potassium deficiency, the physician can prescribe absorbable magnesium, or, better, organic silica.

Dr. Charnot also concluded that there is a connection between potassium and decalcification:[16] potassium is a macromineral. The human brain needs potassium to increase or maintain mental alertness. The human body needs twice as much potassium as calcium, making potassium the most prominent mineral in human nutrition. Mental acuity depends on the presence of potassium. Deficiency symptoms include apathy, nervousness, irritability, and disorientation. All kinds of neurological illnesses occur when this vital mineral is missing in the body, including disturbance of the electrical conductivity of the heart.

Massive decrease of potassium in the cell, for whatever reason (in view of the blockage of acidity that usually takes place), is compensated by the increase of calcium taken from the calcium reserves in the bones. This compensating action of calcium and potassium and the problems that arise because of excess in one of these elements (the antagonism of which is fierce) has been known for a long time.

The excess contribution of potassium, when it disappears from the cell, can to a certain degree reestablish the metabolism of calcium to normal levels. On the other hand, everything that can act usefully on calcium metabolism by a process similar to the influence of vitamins A and D on calcium, must indirectly improve the metabolism of calcium itself.

The correct simultaneous contribution of organic silica and potassium can therefore reestablish the normal distribution of calcium in the organism. In this way Charnot obtained the recalcification of the bones and rapid calcification of the tuberculous caverns without supplementing calcium. This observation shows the bone-recalcifying power exhibited by organic silica of vegetable origin in the presence of potassium and without any therapeutic use of calcium. (See also Chapter 5 – Ousting Osteoporosis.) In this connection it is worthwhile to mention that organic silica and potassium occur simultaneously in horsetail!

Amazing Silica Powers
Experiments with guinea pigs have shown that a deficiency in vitamin C suppresses the formation of collagen in the "fibre growth" called fibroblast. It is probable that protoplasmic vegetable silica has regenerative power. It contributes the biologically catalyzing element to start up the fibroblast again, permitting the tissues to regain their tone and elasticity. This mechanism greatly affects the appearance of our skin. (See Chapter 6 – Collagen and The Silica Connection – for further information.)

Silica in Wonderland
The close connection between silica and calcium points to the influence of silica in growth. The unborn human baby manifests an abundant supply of silica in its tissues. This glut of silica serves to meet the tremendous initial demand of the developing organism, in particular the skeleton and

teeth. So mothers-to-be should receive increased amounts of silica through their food or through supplementation or medication.

Another researcher, Cretin,[17] published interesting observations on the improved stature of children born of weak and sickly mothers. Due to supplementary silica added to their food after weaning, these children showed a remarkable increase in size, and also in weight and chest measurements. I will have more to say about silica and childhood.

Now I want to mention an interesting study undertaken in the Sixties in France where research scientist Randoin[18] worked with white rats, the results of which are invincibly conclusive. Rats were chosen that had been on a rachitis-causing diet. Rats with broken femurs were separated into several groups and subjected to diets containing composite minerals to figure out the influence on the callus (new bony tissue) repair. X-rays were taken every seven days. The animals receiving organic, that is, vegetal silica showed extremely rapid calcification from the tenth day onward; the callus was clearly formed. On the twentieth day the repair was complete. It showed calcium density far superior to that in the control group of rats, which did not receive organic silica and showed no evidence of bone tissue fusions.

These observations clearly prove the validity of therapeutic internal use of vegetal silica in traumatic, infectious, or orthopedic bone ailments. The mineral composition of the bone is very favorably influenced by silica.

Silica increases calcium absorption by the bones without calcium supplementation. The daily requirement for an average adult is 10 to 20 mg of organic vegetal silica and two to three times this quantity for therapeutic uses. For the treatment of broken bones, the dosage should be much higher. (See Chapter 5 – Picking a Bone With Calcium) for details on bone maintenance.)

A Question of Balance

Everywhere Professor Kervran looked, he found an imbalance of the elements that could not be reconciled with the existing law of the conservation of matter. The two sides of the balance sheet just couldn't be made to add up, a familiar nightmare of accountants all over the world. An aunt of mine comes to mind. She is the accountant for an agricultural co-op. Once she worked late into the night for seven days to find a $1.00 imbalance in her books. Because her home was far away from work and our family lived near her place of work, she slept at our house during that week. Out of sympathy my mother offered her the dollar. "After all, the co-op is turning over millions each month. So what's a dollar?" my mother reasoned. "Well," my aunt explained patiently, "that's not possible. The books must balance." That is solid reasoning for bookkeeping, but how can we balance science and nature?

The sciences of biology (life study) and chemistry (matter study) had to merge into the separate, new science of biochemistry when it came to explaining the behavior of living matter. Only in this way could the "books" be balanced. The merger seems to have carried a small prejudice (that extra dollar!) from chemistry into the new bioscience. While many interactions of living matter are produced by traceable chemical reactions, in biochemistry the unperceived phenomenon of transmutation takes place.

According to Kervran, the chemistry of the living organism is essentially different from the chemistry in the lab. Chemists require very high temperatures and often great pressures to create certain reactions. Similar reactions can occur inside the living body at much lower temperatures.

The human organism makes this possible through living enzymes that catalyze endless biological reactions inside the body. The elements involved in these transmutations are all highly unstable – but so is life! We will examine enzyme action more closely later.

Meanwhile, classical chemistry or even nuclear physics, studies dead matter using a type of analysis called *in vitro*. This type of analysis, Kervran reasons, can neither understand nor explain living biological transmutation – so it denies its existence. Though change is the only constant in life, many noteworthy biologists, chemists and physicists like to cling to the familiar laws of yesteryear. This is especially regrettable when they base their generally understandable scientific reluctance on findings that are unrelated to life and living functions. Goethe said, "We are used to see that man ridicules and despises what he cannot understand."[19] The evidence in favor of biological transmutation is, according to Kervran, irrefutable and has been confirmed often. Biological transmutation, he deducts, is a fact of life.

"Physicists do not deny the presence of an energy that maintains life, but for them this energy comes from what the organism takes in from its surrounding outside medium. They do not realize the great flaw in their argument!" The principle of entropy, Kervran holds, has never been applicable to biology. "It was formed only for closed systems having no exchange with the outside; therefore the concepts of entropy and negentropy (negative entropy) have no significance when there is an exchange with the outside medium," says Professor Kervran.[20]

Entropy, of course, is the energy of a thermodynamic system that is unavailable for work. Some energy always converts to heat instead and escapes to outside the system under consideration, as, for instance, within the thermodynamic system of a running car engine. This is why the engine of your car requires constant cooling while you are running your car. Entropy therefore is a measure of the molecular disorder caused by the thermodynamic rundown effect in which steady heat increase occurs within a closed system. Yet in practice, no closed system can exist. Because no matter how well insulated, some energy will escape as heat, leaving the universe in its entirety as the only possible "closed system." Because of this it has been theorized that the physical law of entropy will slowly change the known universe, considered a closed thermodynamic system, into total disorder or chaos. For this phenomenon the term "heat death" was coined.

Kervran, questioning the applicability of entropy to the "human system," goes on to say, "Who is to say in which present-day branch of physics 'mental energy,' the strength of will or character, should be placed?"

It's fitting to look again to Albert Einstein, the most eminent physicist of our time, also one of the wisest. In his research Einstein allowed for scientific doubt, expansion of existing scientific ideas, and an *overriding* God![21]

Well then, that extra dollar might be an *extraordinary* item and can be written off. We have balanced the books. However, to be properly scientific, at the conclusion of this controversial explication, let me repeat: Professor Kervran's biological transmutation explanation regarding the workings of silica is just *one* theory. In the scientific fact of our day, it does not even have the support of the people who hold the world rights for original vegetal silica.

However, the last balancing act of this controversy, Kervran's own, may shed a completely new light on matters. In a discussion of chemical theory at the very end

---

of this book on biological transmutations, Kervran says, "The preceding pages have shown that transmutation of elements in biology is in no way opposed to chemistry. Chemistry is a science which deals with displacements of electrons in the peripheral atomic layers; it is the science of molecules, not of atomic nuclei. The phenomenon I have demonstrated involves an alteration in structural arrangements of atoms induced by enzyme activities in living matter. It takes place within the atomic nuclei; therefore it is a new science, quite distinct from chemistry. Chemistry is only a visible extension of this new science to our perception and it is the application of chemistry, the final stage, that establishes that transmutation occurred."

4

Of Tall Horsetail Extraction

Well-Bred Equisetum arvense

After exploring the very interesting and very challenging, but in many ways still very doubtful hypothesis of Professor Kervran, let us move on to verifiable scientific silica truths.

It is a proven fact that silica plays an important fertilizing role in the plant kingdom. Tests have shown an improvement in cultivation following the addition of silicates. Silica also functions as a vital element in protecting plants against mould penetration, and it has been found to influence the use of other ingredients useful to plant metabolism. A rich supply of natural organic silicates can be found in *Equisetum arvense*, the source of vegetal silica.

Better known as horsetail, spring horsetail, or scouring rush, this perennial grows wild in all temperate zones of our planet. It belongs to a small group of plants known as pteridophyta, which is distinguished as nonflowering and non-seed-bearing. Horsetail thrives on clay-like sandy soils. It occurs mainly in marsh lands but can be found in woods and forests, moist fields, meadows and along the sandy shores of creeks and streamlets. Some varieties have adapted to other environments, living alongside roads and on stony ground. Horsetail has such an awe-inspiring history that a short trip into the distant past will be helpful and electrifying.

Fairy Horsetails

Equisetum arvense first proliferated in the swamps of the Paleozoic or "ancient life" era,* a time span covering an inconceivable 350 million years. During that age the plant reached tree size, with some horsetail trees attaining truly gigantic proportions. The plant is a relative of the so-called "tree ferns" and is known as horsetail fern. Horsetail trees flourished and blanketed the earth in ever greater abundance right into the Pennsylvanian period, 280 million years ago, living during a truly wondrous time. Dragonflies were of colossal dimensions, perhaps causing the medieval and Chinese notions of dragons?

Acquiring Horsetail Sense

Even if today's horsetail is more "down to earth," it fascinated me when I was a boy – and still does. I grew up on the edge of a forest where E.arvense prospered. Studying this fascinating herb for many hours, I discovered that the plant grows two kinds of stems. Fertile stems without chlorophyll grow up to eight inches tall. They are brown in color and appear first but dry up quickly after maturity.

Soon after sterile pale green stems with stepped sheaths follow. The green stems are the food-producing element. The stems consist of sectional tubes that pull apart easily.

---

* The era of geological history between the Mesozoic and the Precambrian, characterized by the development of invertebrates and the appearance of reptiles, amphibians and seed-bearing plants.

Sections fit into one another much like parts of a pipeline. The Germans call the plant aptly "Schachtelhalm," which translates into "stacked spire," a good descriptive name for the stem. Because the individual sections resemble miniature pine trees, horsetail is known also as "meadow-pine."

In its whorled arrangement, horsetail differs from all other *pteridophytes*.* Similarly to mushrooms and ferns, horsetails reproduce by the formation of spores, single-celled structures of microscopic protoplasm. They in turn can produce a new organism. No ancestral or fossil form known to date is more primitive than the living horsetail.

A Polished Breed

Springtime horsetail, especially rich in silica, goes by many other names, some of which are: shave grass, horse willow, horsetail rush, field horsetail, bottlewort, bottle brush, scouring rush. The French call it queue-de-chat (cat's tail) or prele des champs or petite prele. Another German name for it is Zinnkraut, referring to pewter or tin that was scrubbed clean with horsetail, taking advantage of the abrasive qualities of the plant. As is evident from these names, the plant was once used widely for scouring.

Tracing the Elements

Horsetail contains more than ten interesting trace elements including potassium, manganese, copper and zinc in noticeable quantities, but foremost silica, present in two forms:

- Interposed or insoluble silica for plant maintenance, stem strength and physical support. This silica is supposed to play no physiological or therapeutic role in the human organism.

---

* In former classifications, members of *Pteridophyta*, a subdivision on the plant kingdom, coordinate with thallophytes, bryophytes and spermatophytes, including the ferns and fern allies.

- Original vegetal silica, which is naturally chelated (complexed) with some organic products, and can be assimilated by man. It has therapeutic properties according to many authors on silica research. The two species richest in soluble silica are giant horsetail (*E. telmateia*) and field horsetail (*E. arvense*). In spite of the difficulty in distinguishing quantitatively the mineral form of this silica from organic silica, Kervran recommends harvesting horsetail only during its active growing phase in spring when the plant engages in transforming its mineral silica into organic silica.

This does not mean that the total silica content is at its maximum in spring or early summer. On the contrary, it is at its lowest, but almost all is in organic form then. On the other hand, after the growing season silica content is very high but composed almost exclusively of mineral silica.

Individual concentration of the various elements varies, depending on climate, soil and season. It has been suggested by some researchers (King and Davison) that horsetail gains its soluble silica through the intervention of an enzyme, silicatase, which is secreted from the roots of the plant and can dissolve silica from grains of quartz. While silica in the soil is an indispensable nutritional element for the development of horsetail plants, the enzyme theory must yet be proven.

There are many other constituents in horsetail. Among these, some play also a major role in the therapeutic efficacy of the plant:

- The flavonoids (0.2 to 0.5 percent) such as quercitin
- The phenolic acids (chlorogenic, caffeic acids)
- Organic acids such as citric and fumaric acid
- The sterols (beta-sitosterol)

According to their chemical structure, it appears (subject to further scientific demonstration) that both the flavonoids and the phenolic acids contained are among the constituents that allow the formation of the wonderful chelates.*

It is most interesting to find out that these other native constituents, mainly the flavonoids, are present in the plant or its whole aqueous extract with silica in correct proportional quantities. The chelates thus formed by nature allow a tremendous increase of the solubility of silica in water, which is also the main constituent of the human body. Still, being unstable, their titration** as such looks problematic, compared with the titration of silica on the one hand, and of the related flavonoids on the other.

Traces of some alkaloids are also present in *Equisetum arvense*. A species akin to *Equisetum arvense*, *Equisetum palustre*, contains more alkaloids, which may be considered toxic, such as palustrine.

To avoid any risk of confusing the species, which look alike when in the dry state or when separated or blended, it is important to verify the absence of alkaloids through adapted scientific methods, such as chromatography, applied to the dried herb. Such verification assures that there can be no risk of misuse or adulteration.

---

* Chelates of silica are chemical links between a molecule of silicic acid and several other atoms within the same organic molecule.
** An analytical procedure for the determination of reactive capacity of a solution. It consists of adding a reagent in small portions of known volume to a known volume of a solution until a desired end point (a color change in an indicator or in the reactants) indicating a known degree of reaction is obtained. It is widely used in quantitative analysis.

Horsetail Powerhealing

Formerly, according to Fournier,[23] horsetail extract used in equal parts with sage in a foot bath was considered very effective against perspiration. Horsetail tincture, applied to the skin surface and used as a daily deodorant possesses identical properties. At least one researcher, Professor Weiss[24] of the University of Berlin, recommends extract of horsetail baths for rheumatism, chronic eczema, neurodermic ailments, circulatory problems, and edema due to of phlebitis and fractures. The entire plant can be used in a decoction as a source of minerals. In homeopathy, a tincture of the fresh plant is administered for cystitis, anuresis and pulmonary tuberculosis.

In previous centuries horsetail tincture or tea served as a mouth wash and gargle for infections such as tonsillitis. It has been in medicinal use since the sixteenth century, a positive sign that it proved beneficial to healing and in preventive therapy.

There are few herbs that equal horsetail:
• As a diuretic – Huchard and Breitenstein[25] noted an average increase of 30 percent in urination. The diuretic effect was confirmed in 1981 by researcher Valliere.
• As a hemostatic.[26]
• And as a vulnerary to heal wounds.

For many centuries horsetail was also used with good results to normalize irritations in cystitis and other bladder and urethral tract obstructions and in the treatment of gout. Still, be careful of any direct (unprocessed) internal use of the plant because excessive doses can lead to poisoning, and also to internal damage from the scraping effect. So ground horsetail powder, sometimes offered in capsule form, that was not extracted by the safe water evaporation method, should not be taken internally.

Of Aqueous Extraction

A word of caution – if you want to gather horsetail herbs on your own: organic vegetal silica should be made by following a method developed by Professor Kervran[27] so that there is no quartz residue. Properly extracted, it yields the maximum concentration of natural vegetal silicates. Such a pure extract is equivalent to approximately five times its weight in dried horsetail.

Never confuse vegetal silica with merely ground-up or powdered horsetail herb. Simply to grind the harvested herb into a fine powder can cause gastric irritation or similar undesirable side effects, because the abrasive quality remains. Ordinary horsetail preparations can be used for polishing and scouring pots and pans, but don't ingest merely powdered or ground-up horsetail. Prepare silica powder on your own only if you also have the know-how and tools to separate and isolate the silica contents by proper water extraction method, removing any unwanted ingredients or impurities.

5

Picking a Bone With Calcium

No Life Without Silica

In 1939, the Nobel Prize winner for chemistry, Professor Adolf Butenant,[28] proved that life as we know it cannot exist without silica. According to research conducted at Columbia University in 1972, silica is an essential nutrient and must be supplied continuously from food sources.

Silica plays an important role in many body functions and has a direct relationship to mineral absorption. The average human body holds approximately seven grams of silica, a quantity far exceeding the figures for other important minerals such as iron. Both iron and silica are body-essential, meaning they are needed for carrying out ongoing metabolic work that is vital to life. Both elements must be continuously supplied. Silica shares with iron the classification of *trace element*. This label distinguishes such elements from the major elements like the macromineral calcium, which is present in the body in much larger quantities. True to life, here too, quantity is no indication of quality – macrominerals and trace elements are equally important to vitality.

Healing Animals

Many studies that prove the favorable influence of vegetal silica on the development of animals have been undertaken. As I mentioned in Chapter 3 (Silica in Wonderland), silica is essential to the development of the skeleton and the mineralization of bone in rats. Silica's absence results in skeletal deformities.

In chickens, besides its obvious role in creating egg shells, silica also is essential for the formation of the skeleton, the comb and feathers.

Rabbits easily develop atheroma if given a high cholesterol diet. In atherosclerotic rabbits, it can be shown that to a high degree silica prevents the formation of atheromatous plaques on the aorta.[29]

Mineral Supermarket

Mobility in mineral exchanges is characteristic of silica. Its sensitiveness and its role in the general defense of the connective tissues, where it forms "bridges" between oxygen and silicon, is unique. Because of oxygen's volatility, this is the first barrier to the degenerative process, and this is where silica plays a fundamental role.

Hormonal disturbances in the human organism are often due to a calcium-magnesium imbalance. Several studies have shown that silicon can restore this delicate balance. Silicon also benefits the assimilation of phosphorus. It thus may be considered to be a catalyst in the use of other elements.

Ousting Osteoporosis

Replacing calcium with silica, nature's perfect bonesetter, is useful in the treatment of osteoporosis. This much-feared disease occurs mainly in aging people and is more prevalent in females. It can lead to the so-called hump-back. The unsightly hump is caused by brittle bones that lack calcium. Osteoporosis attacks women primarily after menopause. More women are dying of fractures caused by osteoporosis than of cancer of the breast, cervix, and uterus combined. But let me tell you why silica supplementation, not calcium, is the answer.

Osteoporosis occurs less frequently in populations whose foods and eating habits are simple when compared to our nutritional abundance. What mechanisms protect these populations? Many individuals and population groups consume lower amounts of calcium than recommended, apparently without any ill effect. Betty Kamen, Ph.D.,[30] reports on some areas in Mexico where the preparation of maize tortillas involves the addition of lime, making the tortillas higher in calcium. Yet there are no reports of differences in the rate of growth of children in these areas compared to growth rates in areas where the lime in the tortillas is omitted. According to calcium supplementation theory, there should be!

She compares these findings to some regions of the Kalahari Desert, a region of the world I truly love. I lived there, married there, and still have friends there. Kalahari well water adds an additional 100 to 200 mg of calcium per day to the diets of people who regularly drink from these wells. Yet the development of children in an area some distance away, who drink from wells where the water is not as calceous, does not differ at all, although they take in much less calcium. So who benefits from extra calcium?

This led Kamen to the conclusion that the presence or absence of calcium from the diet has no impact on bone composition. She goes on to say, "Many foods are rich in calcium. Calcium abounds. Why should anyone require more? Why is it being added to everything from whole wheat bread to diet cola, and, in England, even to milk? If there is any protective value in calcium supplementation, the reasons for it are yet to be clarified." Kamen learned this during an International Symposium on Osteoporosis, held in Denmark in the eighties.

In osteoporosis there is thinning of the bones due to insufficient production of the surrounding protein medium in which calcium salts first deposit. A lack of calcium in the bone matrix leads to enlargement of canals and spaces in the bones, giving the bones a porous, thinned appearance. The weakened bone becomes fragile and may be broken by some minor injury. The bones may even fracture from normal pressure or stress. Unfortunately, there may be no apparent symptoms until some fragile bone fractures with only slight provocation, such as a minor jolt.

Meanwhile, medical science has agreed that poor nutrition over a period of many years, and possibly poor assimilation through the diet, are major contributing factors. Treatment must include helping calcification. But once the disease has manifested itself, this may be difficult to do. Excessive intake of minerals like calcium over a long period (longer than required for healing broken bones!) may harm the kidneys, especially in a patient whose mobility is obviously reduced. It follows that we must change our focus to timely prevention.

Some medical circles recommend drinking water with fluoride content and a 'new' hormone called calcitonin that can decrease the amount of calcium excreted in urine. Calcitonin also usually increases absorption of calcium by the intestines, and thus preserves bone strength by decreasing mineral losses. Unfortunately these "cures" are too drastic and may result in ill health. Newer findings show that fluorine can cause cancer while hormone treatments can cause several unwanted side effects.

Another questionable treatment popular in the United States is hormone replacement therapy using oral estrogen for menopausal women, although estrogen treatment is still experimental. Dr. Martin Milner of Portland, Oregon, says that although estrogen as a hormone affects the bone matrix, he would prefer to offer menopausal women a chance to maintain healthy bones on their own. Says he, "First, let's determine a woman's adequacy to manufacture estrogen, and give her the kind of nutritional support that will encourage her to continue to make that estrogen."[31]

The bone growth process includes adding calcium plus increasing collagen to give bones their required hardness, yet also flexibility. Silica is essential for both hardness and flexibility. An important study, conducted at the School of Public Health, University of California, shows that silica-supplemented bones have a 100 percent increase in collagen over low-silica bones. Test animals maintained on low silicon diets exhibited impaired growth, disturbances of bone formation, and pigmentation of frontal teeth.

The Dirty Dozen
Warning Symptoms of impending Osteoporosis:
1. You were informed you have trouble absorbing calcium.
2. You were told you have not enough hydrochloric acid in your stomach.
3. You undergo premenstrual-tension syndrome.
4. You cannot tolerate milk or exhibit other gastro-intestinal tract intolerance.
5. You had coeliac illness as a youngster.

6. You are confounded by habitual burping.
7. You have had estrogen/progesterone difficulty.
8. You have had liver or kidney problems.
9. You have significant loss of teeth or far too many cavities.
10. You frequently encounter cramps in calf muscles during sleep or during workouts.
11. You often suffer from lower back pain.
12. You have lost height.

It has been popular to recommend calcium supplementation as a preventive and curative treatment. A better way to prevent and alleviate this crippling disease could be regular supplementation of organic vegetal silica. This has also been reported to neutralize the detrimental effects of aluminum in osteoporosis, and also in Alzheimer's disease. For purposes of remineralization of damaged bones, it is recommended to ingest of one to two teaspoons of organic silica daily. This small amount of vegetal silica dissolves easily in half a glass of lukewarm water that can be taken in small sips. Bones are made up mainly of phosphorus, magnesium and calcium but they also contain silica. It is silica that is responsible for the depositing of minerals into the bones, especially calcium! It speeds up the healing of fractures, as mentioned previously. Silica also reduces scarring at the site of a fracture.

A Natural High
Silica is essential for fetal development and growth. Even so, children have been taught for years that the first essential mineral is calcium. I remember well receiving calcium supplementation as a growing boy. The doctor insisted on it especially because I had never been breast-fed. Normally babies receive calcium in mother's milk. This is vital to the growing human body, vital to the function and regulation

of the heart, vital to muscular activity, vital to the nervous system, and vital to bone formation, growth and maintenance.

However, I think it is even more remarkable that there are high levels of silica at birth and in the young child, yet little calcium in the newborn baby. After that, with each succeeding year, silica is rapidly decreasing while calcium is increasing. Why should this be so? It is due to an internal body mechanism that hastens the aging process; because poor assimilation of silica is, particularly in the elderly, a factor in silica deficiency! We will touch upon the aging mechanisms in greater detail, but let's first consider the ingredients for youthful looks.

Horsetail

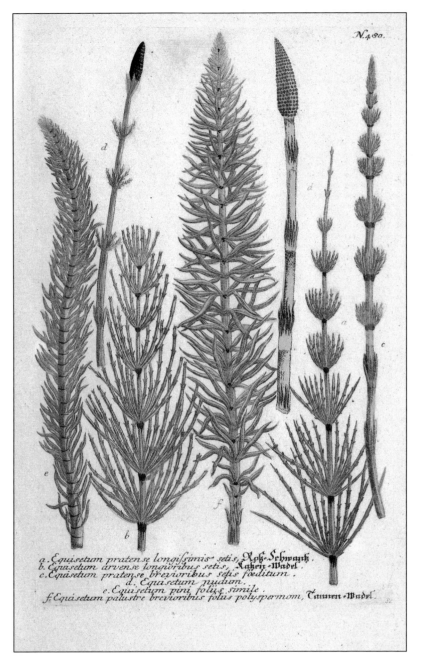

Six species of Horsetail *Equisetum*
Reproduction of an original Lithograph from the collection of
Harlan Lahti — Vancouver, Canada

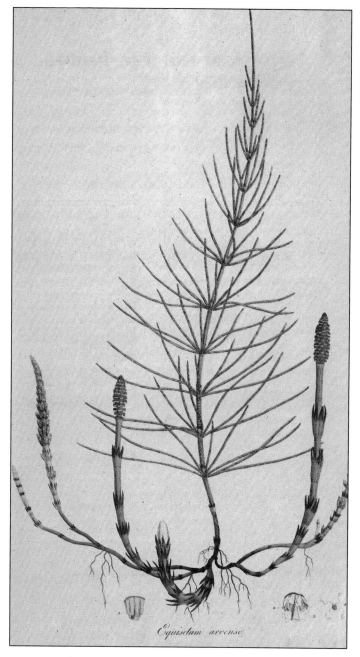

Equisetum Arvense — Spring Horsetail
Reproduction of an original Lithograph from the collection of
Harlan Lahti — Vancouver, Canada

Professor Louis Kervran

Louis Kervran, a French professor, began studying trace elements including silicon in 1949. A method of deriving a silicon extract from horsetail rushes using only water, with no chemicals or solvents, was developed and patented. As a result of this revolutionary technique, a water-soluble silicon extract was made available for continued research and new applications. Clinical tests are constantly being carried out in different countries to provide further insights into this preparation's positive effects.

6

Nature's Internal Cosmetic

Beauty More Than Skin-Deep

The search for beauty clearly leads to the enormous number of beauty products offered. Appearance is so important that department stores dedicate their most visible and accessible store area, the expensive ground floor, to the sale of cosmetics. Is beauty a lotion that we can rub into our skin or a cover we paint on it? Is beauty only skin-deep? The answer plainly is no.

I intend to show that vitality and life, which are so often lost as the years accumulate, can be naturally maintained or even restored to your skin. If you believe that the great screen beauties are constantly under the surgeon's knife for face lifts, think again. They are better advised. They know a secret formula that they apply and practice as a way of living. It is a nutritional formula that helps retard the degenerative process of connective tissue. Tissue degeneration accelerates due to aging when connective tissue develops an increasing inability to retain moisture if left unassisted.

Let's face it, nothing is as comforting as hearing how good we look. A good-looking complexion and beautiful hair make one feel wonderful on the inside, because they bestow self-confidence.

Well, I have some great news! There is an internal cosmetic that also will reflect advantageously on your outside appearance. The secret to how it works is hidden under your skin in a tissue called collagen. I discovered an excellent book, well worth reading, written by Stella Weller, published by Thorson's Publishing Group under the title *Silky, Smooth and Strong*. In her book Weller explains the role collagen plays in beauty in "glowing" details.

Collagen and the Silica Connection

Connective tissue consists of collagen, elastin and mucopolysaccharides, mucous carbohydrates which help moisture retention. Mucopolysaccharides are also called glucosaminoglycanes. Their ability to retain moisture keeps the connective tissue "bouncy" and has obvious importance in the prevention of premature aging. All these important molecules house large quantities of – wouldn't you know it – silica. Collagen, largely made up of silica, is the "glue" that holds us together. Provided our body is enabled to produce enough of it and of glucosaminoglycane, collagen will keep us young-looking.

Our cells' molecules constantly undergo chemical reactions. In the process, highly volatile, broken-off pieces of molecules – free radicals – form. These latch on to other molecules, and in so doing damage protein and enzymes, DNA or RNA. Free radicals also cause cross-linkage, the binding together of large molecules that contribute to the aging process. Cross-linking incapacitates. Cross-links form in the collagen or the connective tissue that binds cells together. Even DNA, nestled in the haven of the cell's nucleus, cannot escape cross-linkage. Destruction of collagen can be devastating to healthy body cells. Let's take a closer look.

Your skin is your largest organ. It has two layers. The medical or proper term for the uppermost layer is epidermis. It is the pliable yet tough boundary between you and the environment. It serves to keep water in the tissues that lie underneath. Without this outer barrier, the body would dry up quickly, the water would evaporate, and remember, we consist mainly of water.

Just below the epidermis lies the second layer called the corium or dermis, which is divided into two sub-layers. The first, the papillary layer, contains blood vessels and sensitive nerve endings. The second, the reticular layer, contains oil glands and hair follicles. It is in the dermis that we find lots of collagen and elastic fibres. Of course, collagen also forms in other organs and in your bones, tendons and muscle tissue. The condition of your collagen determines the appearance and condition of your skin. In young-looking skin, the collagen is healthy. As a result your skin appears soft and smooth. In time collagen can lose its elasticity. As it deteriorates, the support of the skin weakens too. Your skin loses its shape and resiliency.

It is collagen that normally "snaps" the skin back into place after it has been stretched. Try it on your skin. Pull the skin up between two fingers, hold it for a moment and let go suddenly. It will "jump" back, even against gravity. Collagen plays such an important role in the appearance of skin, and therefore in our looks, that it has become popular to inject animal collagen under the skin to remove wrinkles and facial lines. While such treatment does the trick, it introduces a foreign substance into the body, and consequently is a harmful procedure. Some people are even allergic to animal collagen. People suffering from connective tissue disorders such as arthritis should not undergo collagen treatment. Besides, the beautifying effect of "artificial" collagen doesn't last. What will work?

There is a stimulating new product on the market that can produce astonishing results. The truth is that for maintaining healthier and longer-lasting collagen a good silica supplementation program works far better. If you regularly follow a silica regimen, your skin will keep its young look. Just don't expect instant results. So it is a good idea to start organic vegetal silica supplementation years before the collagen in your body has deteriorated to the point where it shows in the wrinkles on your face and body.

Research conducted by Dr. Klaus Schwartz[33] supports this finding. Another research team, Zeller and Odier,[34] also attributes a primary role to silica in the defense of connective tissue. Silica works in the connective tissue not in its free form, but as a salt of silicic acid known as silicate orologosilicate. The silica which you ingest converts into this compound inside the body.

The skin on your face needs special attention, wrinkles being a most visible problem. Wrinkles are the result of years of stress and drying out of the supporting collagen. Besides silica supplementation, a sun screen applied to your skin when you are out in the sun will help keep wrinkles away. Remember, ultraviolet radiation will penetrate clouds and reach your skin even on overcast days. I have lived in many countries and am always impressed with the way the natives of hot, sunny climates dress. They cover themselves from head to foot, particularly females. They know how to escape the sun!*

Only northerners, who adore the sun when it finally feels

---

* I'm talking about over-exposure to the sun. Approximately 20 minutes of full-body sun exposure per day is actually healthy.

warm again after the long cold winter, habitually over-expose themselves to the hot sun. Here too, it takes years before your skin finally capitulates under the sun's constant onslaught. This risk of cumulative damage is another good reason to protect yourself with silica supplementation.

Give your skin all the help it can get against excessive radiation, no matter from which source. There has been concern lately about excessive radiation emanating from power lines and sub-stations that transmit electricity and from the electrical appliances in our homes.

Into the Last Stretch

Formulas for external application that contain strong concentrations of soluble silica extract have proven effective in the prevention and repair of stretch marks. Under controlled test conditions an average 70 percent success rate in repair was obtained, and a one percent success in diminishment of recent stretch marks.

When purchasing an anti-wrinkle cream, read the label and make sure it mentions silica. A skin care program should be based on a Kervran-formulated horsetail-derived silica. Such skin care delivers silica nutrients to the entire body, not just the face.

If your skin cream does not contain silica, you could simply add bulk vegetal silica from your health food store to your skin cream before applying it to your skin. A good skin cream to do this with would be an essential fatty acid (EFA) based cream. Following such a program ensures that you supply sufficient silica to your system from the inside out and from the outside in.

Racing Against Inflammation

Cellulitis is the medical term for an inflammation of cellular tissue. The condition is a complex phenomenon of proliferation and swelling of fatty cells (adipocytes) that leads to tearing of the connective tissue. In such cases weight reduction becomes indispensable. Horsetail extract administration has a positive supportive action in the healing process.

A Horsetail by Any Other Name
Ingestion of organic vegetal silica, if taken regularly, can be a natural deodorizer. This is exciting news for all who are in close contact with other people during work hours or while socializing.

Bouncy Skin
Aging skin often is less elastic. This correlates with the theory that silica has an elastogenic function. Researchers Holt and Osborne[3] showed that silicic acid diminishes permeability in the skin, making it less susceptible to deterioration.

Long term organic vegetal silica supplementation will normalize skin and bestow younger-looking skin. Silica will lend suppleness and elasticity to your skin which are lost over the years or from bad dietary habits and an unhealthy lifestyle. Your skin will regain elasticity and tone. Striking results have been obtained, particularly with striae (linear, parallel stripes). Striae can appear following pregnancy.

Silica can help to relieve symptoms resulting from undernourished skin. Such symptoms can include itching, rashes, acne, abscesses, calluses, warts, eczema, benign skin tumors, bed sores, and leg ulcers. Silica will also accelerate healing of insect bites, injuries, wounds, burns and frostbite. Silica acts as a biocatalyst and can be added to the bath to stimulate the healing of chronic eczema. To strengthen skin and increase resistance to skin ailments, use silica internally and apply it externally. You can maintain the firmness and tone that were originally intended for your skin by your genes.

Assuring adequate and regular intake of vegetal silica can influence the entire state of your body. Besides the obvious health benefits, you can reap the reward of increased beauty, which your mirror will soon reveal. Supplementation works with your regular skin care and a balanced diet that includes plenty of the foods rich in silica. I have listed these foods for you in Chapter 10 (Horsetail Cooking). Do not forget adequate rest and regular exercise. Like all organs, in order to work well, your skin needs the right nourishment and exercise. That includes laughter, a healthy exercise for your face. The cells in the base layer of the skin where cells are formed become more vigorous with exercise. Keeping physically fit also will help to maintain the body's manufacture of other substances needed to produce elastic fibres.

Tough as Nails

Your nail plates are complex protein structures that grow four to five millimeters per month on average. In cases of deficiency, the rate of growth slows. So your fingernails can be the first indicators of a silica deficiency. If they are brittle or show a dark, abnormal surface, they deserve closer examination. Demineralization of the nails precedes by far any decalcification of the bones. It is possible therefore to start silica therapy in time to prevent bone loss.

Lack of silica is common in people suffering from degenerative conditions like osteoporosis. In Chapter 5 (Picking a Bone With Calcium), I review this devastating disease in greater detail. Arthritis and atherosclerosis are accompanied by similar silica deficiency states. The French researchers Kervran, Charnot and Monceaux[34] found that with silica supplementation, fragile nails became normal within a short period. Silica will beautify the appearance of your nails and improve their hardness, making them shinier and less prone to breaking.

Hair That Glows

Hair is nature's greatest beauty enhancer. It makes us sexually attractive and serves to protect us. Hair deserves to be babied. Already in the first edition of this work I praised the effects of silica on hair. By now you should be able to find a suitable silica shampoo that contain aqueous horsetail-extract in your health food store. Using a good silica shampoo should be part of your ongoing hair care program for revitalizing hair.

If your hair is damaged, a four-month hair restoration program should include a silicated protein hair conditioner, hopefully one that is fortified with bee pollen extract. You can create your own mix, using your favorite shampoo as a base, or obtain a suitable conditioner from your health food store. A four-month regime promises increased hair growth. Following such a silica hair care program will leave you with thicker, fuller and healthier hair. Why not check out suitable hair care products on your next visit to your health food store?

Studies done in Russia have revealed a measurable slowing of hair loss through silica therapy. It appears that silica added to shampoos helps to prevent baldness, stimulates healthier hair growth and assures beautiful shine, luster and strength. Since organic vegetal silica will completely dissolve, you can easily add it to your regular shampoo if you cannot locate silica shampoo in your store.

Adding silica to my shampoo for six years has helped. I have effectively contained hair loss. I started to lose hair in my thirties and the loss accelerated once I reached the age of forty. I saw myself balding quickly. Then, in 1987, I started silica treatment and six years later, in 1993, I could proudly report that I have checked hair loss – seemingly permanently. At least I have not lost any more hair since 1987. You'll see what I mean when you see me – just look at my latest book cover.

Now I plan to be working on regrowing lost hair through the complete silica shampoo therapy offered by combining a silica hair care program with internal silica supplementation. The most effective means of hair care is regular external application, complemented with periodic internal supplementation. Following such a dual approach formula will assure optimal hair care.

Teeth and Gums
By hardening the enamel, silica prevents cavities and preserves teeth. Silica also prevents bleeding gums and gum atrophy and recession that cause loosening of teeth, which could ultimately lead to tooth loss. Vegetal silica effectively fights caries (ulceration and the decay of a bone or of a tooth) and inflammation. If possible purchase a toothpaste containing silica or, if you can't find one, use the content of a silica capsule and mix it with your regular toothpaste.

There is no doubt that the restorative effects of silica will be most noticeable on your hair, skin, nails and teeth. Even so, skin and hair require silica essentially for the same purpose as do other tissues. As we have seen, the supporting collagen underneath skin physically lends it its elasticity and beauty. Collagen owes that quality to silica, which is why I can publicly proclaim that a beautiful complexion is more than skin deep.

7

Silica and the Aging Riddle

Youthful Aging

Have you ever caught yourself thinking, "My laugh lines are starting to look like a Chinese fan. When did those spare tires about my hips emerge? And I'm only 35?" Stop being afraid of growing older! Old age does not have to mean infirmity, ugliness, undesirability. With an emphasis on proper nutrition you will surely slow the degenerative processes even if you can't stop the passing of the years. The earlier you begin, the more you will benefit. Still, it is never too late to begin rejuvenating habits like silica supplementation.

You might have heard the astrologers' claim that Capricornians live in reverse, getting younger as they grow older. Well, silica is the Capricorn of the mineral world. Better yet, silica has the added advantage that it is scientifically proven. Organic vegetal silica has a definite rejuvenating effect. I'll explain. When our bodies are young, they contain lots of silica and little calcium. With each succeeding year, the silica content of body tissue usually decreases while calcium content increases. It is silica that maintains flexibility and bounce. It's Mother Nature's secret behind that famous baby bounce that we are taught to associate only with youth. Isn't this tremendous news? Here at last is a scientific, effective and essentially very simple method for life extension.

Consider your immune system whose gradual deterioration relates directly to the degenerative process called aging. Supplementing with organic vegetal silica stimulates the body's defense mechanisms. While young, our bodies have resilient skin. Silica can maintain for us or quickly restore the resiliency of our skin. Original vegetal silica's effects on collagen result in a pulling together of tissues.

This reminds me of a riddle. "What is it that everybody wants to become but nobody wants to be?" The answer is "old." There is an obvious ambivalence in society's attitude to getting old. It can easily be overcome by realizing that getting "old" – as in maturing – is not synonymous with premature aging!

The true goal in life is to mature. One should never attempt to stop maturing, because attaining maturity is the reward of a vital growth process that, at its best, involves body, mind, and soul. On the other hand, the similar-sounding, but essentially different process of premature aging can be slowed; who knows, if science keeps advancing at its dizzying pace, maybe even stopped? You see, we really want to season, we just don't want to grow infirm in body and mind. So for a moment at least let me concentrate on disabilities and bodily conditions that people fear most in old age. Let's destroy a myth!

Food for Thought
You don't have to fear loss of mental ability until you are well into your eighties or even older. To avoid brain calci-

fication, just be sure to keep mentally active. Stimulate and exercise your mind continuously, just as you do your body. Remember that a wholesome body and sound mind require a natural balance. Don't worry, though, if you are not a born philosopher.

Try brain teasers such as crossword puzzles, participate in continuing education programs, play chess. Then again, maybe this is the right time for you to go back to school and finish that program you have been dreaming about. Do whatever you like best, but keep your brain thinking. It's only when you stop using your mental faculties that you start growing old.

Why not supplement your diet with ginkgo biloba if you think your memory capacity requires improvement? I do, just to be on the safe side. If you suspect Alzheimer's however, things are getting serious and it may be a good idea to check for excessive mercury in your system. My book *Eliminating Poison in Your Mouth** details the best way to check this out and provides new approaches to overcoming mind-robbing mercury amalgam toxicity.

Hair Repair
Massaging your scalp regularly and controlling harmful or excessive physical and mental stress with regular exercise and positive thinking will also help keep your hair in good repair. Adding silica-rich foods to your diet or supplementing with organic vegetal silica helps protect your hair and restore shine.

Adding silica to your favorite shampoo will normalize hair loss (i.e., stop premature hair loss) and add shine. You can do this simply: dissolve two tablespoons of bulk organic

---

* 1991, Alive Books, Burnaby, BC

vegetal silica in a few ounces of hot water and then add the mixture to your shampoo. The results are terrific.

I know of only one company who package a bulk organic vegetal silica suitable for adding to your shampoo. You should be able to find this Kervran product in your health food store. If you cannot find a bulk silica in your store, ask the supplier, Flora Manufacturing & Distributing Ltd., to direct you to a source or write to me and I will assist you.

If you are wondering how to select the right shampoo for your hair, try out different brands from the shelves of your health food store until you find the one that is good to your scalp. It took me several years of trial and error to come up with the best shampoo for my hair. Always select hair care products that are free of artificial chemicals. Carefully reading the ingredients printed on the label before you purchase a shampoo or conditioner that is new to you will avoid many pitfalls. Then again, you may just prefer to select a ready formulated silica shampoo waiting for you on the shelves of your natural or health food store.

To get a better understanding of your hair, it is a good idea to have a hair analysis done. This will also reveal body levels of toxins, including the deadly mercury I mentioned above. Your naturopathic doctor can obtain an accurate hair analysis for a small fee for you. You can also contact one of the hair analysis labs directly. Many analytical laboratories (let your fingers to the walking in the Yellow Pages) will do accurate hair analysis. The labs will tell you how to submit your hair sample, but remember to request silica values to be included in the analysis. Also request that the read-out of your values is compared to average or normal range values. This helps understanding of the read-out.

Young at Heart

You know what I find sad? In our society 50 percent of people over the age of 65 have problems with their heart. Heart disease is still the Number One Killer. Yet you can prevent heart disease by a proper supplementation program and by controlling your food intake.

Silica has inhibitory effects on coronary disease. Eat silica-rich meals and supplement where necessary. It is vital to reduce total fat intake – no matter the source or kind of fat! You will need some fats though and should favor HDL-rich fats like fresh cold-pressed flaxseed oil instead of your usual salad oil. It tastes better too. Eating nuts helps to obtain healthy fat intake and has statistically been shown to reduce the incidence of heart disease.

Nowadays there is a great selection of cold-pressed oils to choose from. You can find them all at your health food store. To assist your heart muscle even more, avoid undue stress and follow a regular exercise program under the professional guidance of your physician. If you suffer from high blood pressure, avoid salt, red meat and egg yolks in your diet. Add plenty of garlic to your regular diet – there is a good reason why it keeps "vampires" like mosquitoes at bay. (Adding it to pet food will help keep pets and your carpets free of fleas.) Why not consult your naturopath on other healthful means to normalize blood pressure?

The beneficial effects of silica supplementation for your heart can be gleaned by studying the chart on the following page that traces changes in mean silicon content in the human aorta.* The graph delineates average values from people that have not supplemented their diet with silica.

---

* The great artery springing from the left ventricle of the heart.

By now you will not be surprised to learn that the aortas of young people of both genders contain more silica. As can be seen clearly, following a rapid decline through childhood, the curve temporarily stabilizes around the age of ten. After that the curve declines more slowly with advancing age, for some reason maintaining throughout a higher value for the male gender. From this it can be inferred that silica supplementation could be even more important for females. Is there a correlation with osteoporosis here?

Silica and the Aging Riddle

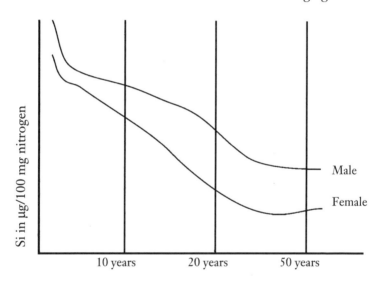

Lung Repair
Air pollution is a big problem for you if, like me, you live in a large city. But there's good news. Even damaged lungs can be repaired over time through remedial action. Organic vegetal silica supplementation helps repair and maintain vital lung tissue.

You also can help your lungs by not smoking* and, in areas of extreme pollution, by filtering your home. In addition, cellular-oxygenation exercises are vital for healthy lungs. That means get out into fresh air as often as possible – time to walk your dog in the park or forest! But avoid the traffic-congested streets. Avoid breathing chemical fumes including gasoline fumes when refuelling any gas tank.

Silicic Muscles

Even the best musculature is no good in the long term without the support of a good, healthy bone structure. This is another area where organic vegetal silica supplementation can be of the utmost benefit. Muscle tone starts to diminish after middle age, but can be largely retained with proper diet and consistent appropriate exercise.

Getting Under Your Skin

Protect the resiliency of your skin with vegetal silica supplementation – it might work wonders. I have expounded on most of the benefits your skin can gain from vegetal silica supplementation in Chapter 6 (Nature's Internal Cosmetic), but here are some more pointers to prevent skin aging. Our bodies continuously lose water through the organs of elimination. The kidneys require large amounts of water first to dilute and then flush out deadly accumulated toxins, primarily uric acid. The body rids itself of this waste product of metabolic activity via the urinary system. Our large skin surface constantly gives off moisture, as do our lungs via mouth and nose. In addition, the body excretes lots of water with stool.

Drink lots of liquids daily. Give preference to non-carbonated glacial or purified water. Water is an essential anti-aging remedy. Six to eight glasses a day helps to mois-

---

* Researchers Zeller and Odier have found that silica acts as a powerful eliminator of nicotine, an organic waste product.

turize your skin and guards against dryness, a forerunner of wrinkles. It is sad to see how so many people, including members of my family, won't provide sufficient water to their systems. Too many people don't drink during the day, and then, at night, drink only unhealthy alcoholic beverages, coffee or black tea.

Moisturizing creams,* fortified with silica and applied frequently, especially after bathing, will help to keep skin cells youthful. Another excellent aid to skin beauty is bathing in a decoction of fresh spring horsetail or, again, adding pure aqueous silica extract to your bath water.

Menopause Free of Stress
During menopause there is a gradual shut-off mechanism that halts estrogen production, the hormone women's bodies need for the health of their bone system. Regular intake of organic vegetal silica helps to prevent many unwanted side-effects of menopause; paramount being the development of osteoporosis (see Chapter 5 – Ousting Osteoporosis). In men, too, the nervous system and glandular network will gradually undergo changes that cause deterioration of vital body functions.

Youth Pills
Apart from organic vegetal silica, which obviously has beneficial effects in the prevention of premature aging, you may wish to consider other minerals and vitamins. Here is a list of supplements that I take regularly. These supplements play a role in preventing premature aging: Vitamin A assists silica in maintaining healthy skin and bones. In addition, it can make you see better in the dark. Beta-carotene can be taken instead of vitamin A.

---

* You can easily stir a thimble-full of bulk organic vegetal silica, a pure extract from spring horsetail, into your favorite moisturizing cream.

Vitamin C, known also as ascorbic acid, it can boost the immune system. It also has antiviral effects. It boosts the production and activity of interferon,* a virus-fighting substance produced by the body. Best of all, vitamin C has been found to aid the assimilation of silica, making it a good idea to take these two supplements together.

Vitamin E protects against cardiovascular disease. Vitamin E is unique in its ability to protect vitamin A and C and fatty acids from oxygen destruction.

Selenium metabolizes free radicals; with vitamin E it breaks free radicals down into harmless components, then promotes their elimination. Many forms of cancer are traceable to a deficiency of this valuable mineral.

Zinc is a powerful booster of the immune system. It helps preserve the senses of taste, smell and vision; the body also needs it for healing wounds (just like silica!). It is necessary in maintaining male fertility and sex drive, and is, in addition, an anti-inflammatory agent. Years ago I used to have a poor sense of smell. Friends would make comments like "lovely cedar fragrance" while driving through a forest. I would look around for a cedar tree because, honestly, I couldn't smell a thing. Since I began supplementing zinc, my olfactory nerve has improved dramatically. So, I can personally vouch for zinc's efficacy in improving the sense of smell.

Reducing Radiation Risks

With the new global easing of tension that greatly reduces the risk of the unthinkable nuclear holocaust, we can relax our enormous fear of radiation sickness. However, some radiation risks remain. There is a level of unavoidable radi-

---

* Stimulating interferon production, and the use of interferon in cancer treatment, are currently being researched.

ation in the atmosphere caused by cosmic rays, sunlight, and the natural breakdown of radioactive elements. Radiation that is released accidentally by nuclear power plants like the recent Chernobyl disaster in the USSR will stay around for a long time to come.

The threatened dissolution of the planet's protective ozone layer through worldwide pollution gives further cause to counter harmful radiation. Think twice before submitting to X-rays too often and avoid prolonged exposure to the hot sun, especially the noon sun in summer. Research has proven that intense radiation contributes to the formation of free radicals. Free radicals do their damage in the way they react with DNA. New research has found that antioxidants, like organic vegetal silica, protect against radiation.

In a world of electrical appliances, most notably computers, we are all increasingly exposed to electric fields that present another source of possibly harmful radiation. Again, silica helps to minimize radiation damage.

A report emanates from my birthplace of Hannover, Germany, in which the well-respected physician and physicist Dr. Hans Nieper describes low frequency electromagnetic therapy for combating disease. The future possibilities of electromagnetic therapy are enormously interesting. Both silica supplementation and low frequency pulsating electromagnetic therapies aid and accelerate wound healing and stimulate bone growth. Their uses may be combined to maximize healing and should be employed in combating arthritis.

Immune System Alert
As the body ages, there is a decrease in lymphocyte or white blood cell response to foreign intruders called antigens. If free radical damage could be reduced, the immune system would remain strong. There is currently specula-

tion among scientists that the key to aging can be found in the deterioration of the immune system.

You can help your immune system stay strong. You have the most immediate control over your own body. At the top of your list of protective measures must be diet and exercise. A balanced diet should include adequate amounts of vitamins, minerals, amino acids, proteins, unsaturated fats like fresh cold-pressed linseed oil, and trace elements. Make regular use of these, but also make sure to keep fat consumption – no matter the source! – low.

You are not sure whether your regular diet contains adequate amounts of vital nutrients? Consider supplementing! If in doubt which supplements to include in a supplementation program, consult your naturopathic or nutritionally oriented physician. You need a guide, such as a hair and blood analysis, to discovering possible mineral deficiencies or excesses and assistance in selecting corrective nutrients accordingly.

Keeping physically active boosts the nutritionally important HDL-type of cholesterol in your bloodstream. HDL helps prevent cardiovascular diseases including heart attacks. The best exercise – and almost everyone can do it – is walking.

Goodbye to Aching Joints

After age forty there is usually some loss of flexibility and suppleness in the joints due to reduced silica in the tissues. Fifty percent of people over the age of sixty-five suffer from joint pain similar to arthritis. It helps to supplement with silica and to keep active with exercise.

Replace your automobile with your feet or bicycle for short distances! Practice prevention. Another worthwhile remedy for aching joints is the root of devil's claw

(Harpagophytum procumbens), a desert plant from Namibia. It has proven anti-rheumatic, anti-arthritic, and anti-inflammatory properties. If you suffer from aching joints, you should read the book *Devil's Claw Root and other natural remedies for Arthritis* by Rachel Carston. This publication is available in specialty book stores and health food stores.

There is lots of calcium and very little silica in the bodies of most older people. Silica supplementation is the answer to certain age-related problems such as soft finger nails, bones and cartilage, or muscle injuries. Bones of most older people do not mend easily due to silica deficiency. Lack of silica in nerve tissues and brain cells can produce poor memory, another well-known symptom of old age.

Older folks often suffer from impaired kidney and bladder function. Well, here is good news. Silica can help prevent kidney stones and heal infections of the urinary tract. It increases excretion of urine by 30 percent,[35] which leads to a flushing of the water-excreting system and restores regular and normal function to these vital organs.*

Another vital organ that is often sluggish and troublesome as we get older is the intestinal tract. The presence of sufficient silica in the intestines will reduce inflammation. It can cause disinfection and absorption in cases of stomach and intestinal catarrh and ulcers. Silica can prevent or clear up diarrhea and its opposite, constipation. Vegetal silica also will help normalize hemorrhoidal tissue and should be used internally and applied externally to hemorrhoids. In regulating and normalizing the bowels, silica has a pleasant side effect: it can alleviate lower back pain, which often

---

* In urinary pathology and gout, F. Decaux and H. Leclerc prescribe a decoction of horsetail obtained from boiling 50g dried plant in 1 litre of water until the liquid is reduced to half (30 minutes), or the liquid extract: approximately 5 to 10g daily.

troubles the elderly. The reason is simple. Much of the lower back pain can be traced to dysfunction of the intestinal tract.

Live to 100!

The Bible* contains many references to great ages attained by the ancients. Today's gerontologists, who specialize in aging and rejuvenation, are predicting ever-increasing life spans. Offer your system foods rich in silica or supplement with aqueous extract from spring horsetail. You can jump on the bandwagon to longevity. For the time being, silica is the latest "magic pill" in the safe form of a nutrient that will help extend the prime of life. The quest for eternal youth, or at least a longer, healthier life goes on.

Meanwhile, centenarians – people who reach the yet seemingly fantastic age of 100 – are the most rapidly growing age group in North America. Just imagine your birthday cake featuring 100 candles. You are asked to blow them out, and still have healthy lungs to do it. To reach that goal, devotion to your family, your social ties, freedom from undue stress, and a healthy desire to survive will be as invaluable to you as silica.

Life is full of wonder. In the year 1992, my wife and I bought our own home – a ten year old townhouse. Gabrielle was ecstatic, dreaming up all kinds of modern improvements. We could hardly wait for the previous occupants to move out. Among junk they left behind for us to sort out, I found a fascinating oddity made of siliceous sinter, i.e., silica sand. At the time, I was writing *Silica – The Amazing Gel*, the companion volume to the book you are now reading. How amazing *Silica – The Amazing Gel* was becoming to me! The silica sinter made up the number 100. The one square foot large siliceous 100 block

* Holy Bible, King James Version, Methuselah, Genesis 5:27.

now stands on my bookshelf. Visitors who spot it never fail to ask, "What is that?" To which I reply, "It's silica spelling the number one hundred. It is an omen of longevity through silica."

8

The Transmuted Healer Within

Therapeutic Vegetal Silica
Silica is indispensable as preventive and curative therapy in
the treatment of several diseases and many degenerative
conditions and processes. Exploratory therapeutic trials
have shown that organo-silicic compounds decrease fat
deposits and speed up the repair of fractures.

Silica therapy has also obtained successful results in
inflammatory rheumatic disorders. Encouraging results
are on record for patients with coronary atherosclerosis,
with an improvement in walking endurance.

Employing a Healing Agent
In bodily functions, silica helps stimulate the immune
system. Vegetal silica not only promotes growth, and bone
and teeth formation, but also plays a vital role in normalizing circulation. A study by Loeper, Loeper and Lemaire in
France has shown that silicon is always present in healthy
blood vessels, but absent from arterial sites that have

become hardened or diseased. Silica helps to regulate high blood pressure (hypertension) too.

Supplementing with silica has been found to decrease vertigo, headaches, tinnitus (buzzing of the ears) and insomnia. By maintaining or restoring the elasticity of lung tissue, silica functions like certain medicines. For instance, it reduces inflammation in bronchitis. It acts as a cough-decreasing agent. Silica tones the upper respiratory tract (nose, pharynx, larynx) and reduces swelling because of its positive action on the lymphatic system.

A field study, conducted in West Germany, in which silica (silicea) was administered, yielded most interesting results. It was made possible by the active cooperation of 73 patients of various ages from 24 to 76. The participants included approximately equal numbers of both sexes. In 64 patients (87.67 percent) very good to satisfactory results were achieved in the treatment of diseases. Conditions ranged from different forms of atherosclerosis (19.18 percent) and illnesses of the digestive system (8.22 percent) to infections of the respiratory tract (31.1 percent), mouth, teeth and gum conditions (12.33 percent) and skin, nail and hair problems, also injuries (17.8 percent).

The following dosages were administered to the group of volunteer patients under the strictest supervision and the exclusion of all other medicines during a treatment period averaging 1.97 months per patient:

Condition	Daily Dosages	Application
1. Atherosclerosis	1	internally
Respiratory tract	tablespoon	dissolved
Connective tissue	1-2 times	in water
Lymphatic system	daily	
Skin, hair, nails		

Condition	Daily Dosages	Application
2. Digestive tract	1 tsp every 2 hours until improvement, then as under 1. above.	internally pure
3. Common cold Mouth, teeth, gums Catarrh Skin diseases Injuries.	1 to 4 times daily directly or as dressing	externally pure or diluted

Tolerance to silica was very good in all patients. There were absolutely no undesirable side effects or attendant symptoms. Only two patients or 2.74 percent showed no measurable improvement over the test period. But in no less than 87.67 percent of cases cited, the results of silica therapy registered as effective. Special mention must be made of the excellent results obtained particularly in the treatment of gum problems.

Diabetes Beaten

According to experiments conducted by P. Gendre and R. Cambar,[41] silica seems to act as a catalyst in relation to the elastase inhibitor. It does so either by activating this inhibitor or by promoting its synthesis by the pancreas. This organ plays an important role in the storage and metabolic regulation of silica.

Several experiments have shown that the therapeutic use of silica improved diabetes in patients. Could this be connected to a decline in silica in the afflicted pancreas, the pancreas of healthy individuals being particularly rich in silica? It is possible, but it also could be caused by the reestablishment of silica levels in the tissues, which are always lowered in the elderly.

Arterial Disease in Retreat

Atherosclerosis is a destructive impedimentation of the major and minor arteries. It is a widespread degenerative process that is unfortunately very common and causes sickness and death. The inner lining of arteries is invaded and fatty substances are deposited that irritate the arterial walls. The process can go undetected for decades before it manifests itself as a disease such as stroke. An obvious cure lies in prevention. Atherosclerotic arteries contain fourteen times less silica than healthy arteries. This was the finding of French researchers[42] after studying 72 adults aged 61 and over. These researchers concluded that silica has an essential protective role in maintaining the elastic connective tissue of the arteries and checking their permeability. In the presence of silica supplementation, elastin fibres did not disappear or dislocate. It would appear that silica inhibits this disease too.

Silica levels in the aorta, a major blood vessel of the heart, diminish very rapidly, though irregularly, with age. Silica has already decreased at the age of 10 years and reaches much lower levels by the age of 40 years. This decrease with age corresponds to the appearance of atheromatic lesions. Infiltration of the connective tissue by plasma lipids becomes possible when the arteries lose their elasticity and become permeable.

This arterial weakness can be diminished by the action of silicic acid, a silica and water compound, according to findings by researchers Holt and Osborne.[43] Their conclusions were independently confirmed by a color diffusion study using rabbits: Silica promotes arterial impermeability to harmful lipids, therefore preventing deposits.

There is no doubt that silica plays a part in preserving the integrity of the arteries. Future research may be directed at discovering the connection between silica salts and the activity of the enzymes that are responsible for the attack on elastic fibres, and thus possibly finding a cure for atherosclerosis.

Immunity to Tuberculosis

This once dreaded disease has not been in the news for some time. Still, there was concern about a tuberculosis breakout in Vancouver, Canada in 1988, and in California in 1992. Extremely infectious, tuberculosis can be spread easily through coughing or sneezing. Apparently medical authorities are again experiencing trouble in containing the disease in affected persons – so it would appear that tuberculosis has not been beaten.

There is a 41 percent lack of silica in tuberculosis patients. In the year 1909, the research team Robin and Marcq[44] proved that the osseous demineralization is connected to silica. This is also true of pulmonary tissue, which loses an average of 50 percent. This loss is connected to diminished silica levels. They prescribed .18 percent silica solution for normal pulmonary tissue and .009 percent for tuberculosis patients. These scientists admitted that the tuberculosis patient takes minerals from his bone tissue that the healthy tissues need to defend themselves against the affected tissues. They concluded that silica is important in the defense against tuberculosis. Modern studies by Charnot[45] confirm the almost total absence of silica in the bones of tuberculosis patients.

Studies by R. de Villanova[46] direct attention to the probable reasons for immunity and predisposition to pulmonary tuberculosis in man and animals. His analysis shows that the silica content in the pulmonary zone is variable and points to geographical tendencies of this disease. The top right lobe – the one most often affected – shows the least quantity of silica with .24 percent. Contrariwise, the top left lobe, which is next in respect of frequency, contains .64

percent. The bottom right lobe, which is the least frequently affected, shows the greatest quantity of silica. Other tests by Royo de Villanova and P. Cassalis[47] confirmed these findings.

In the guinea pig, particularly receptive to tuberculosis infection, the quantity of silica was especially low in all organs and particularly in the lungs. There is extreme lack of silica in animals (cow, guinea pig) that are predisposed to tuberculosis. There is abundance in those (sheep, goat, rat) that are hardly receptive or even resistant. This leads to the belief that silica is an important element in the defense of the organism against tuberculosis infection. It should become a precious medicine in the treatment of this dangerous disease.

Insufficiencies in mineral nutrition were blamed in tuberculosis patients – above all, calcium! This nutrient is definitely important, but we have just seen that silica is more important, because it is silica that is first mobilized for defense. The correct balance between silica and calcium must be maintained to ward off pathological mineral plundering and the displacement of minerals.

A World Without Cancer
In the area of Daun in West Germany[48] there is an extremely low incidence of cancer. In searching out the reasons why the locals should be more fortunate than folks elsewhere, it was discovered that the water from the local Dunmaris well, on emergence from the ground, is unusually high in silica. Cancer patients often suffer a mineral imbalance. The most prominent losses suffered are: silica, magnesium, calcium and iron. Even benign tumors, such as warts, are known to develop mainly during periods of bodily demineralization or shortage of these minerals. They sometimes disappear spontaneously when the mineral imbalance has been corrected.

A French researcher, Leriche,[49] points out that cancers are rare in areas rich in silica, and, contrariwise, frequent in areas rich in calcium but poor in silica. Dr. Charnot,[50] in his observations on bone cancer of the femur, reports that silica has almost disappeared in the tumor zones. According to researcher Remmets[51] of Dortmund, the connective tissue in cancer patients reveals a significant lack in silica content.

A. Robin,[52] and more recently, Zeller, Dupuy de Frenelle[53] and other scientists have established that certain elements of first defense like silica, calcium and magnesium could attach to tumors. Robin showed that it was silica that arrived first at the tumor site, by far outdoing calcium and magnesium. Zeller and Odier[54] ascribe a prime role to silica in the defense against cancer. They find that silica works in the following two ways:
• As a powerful eliminator of organic waste products, particularly urea, uric acid and nicotine.
• As strengthener of the connective tissue, the prime barrier set up by the body to ward off the progression of cancer cells and the degenerative process.

Researcher Luithler[55] found that silica intervenes as a remineralizing agent and plays the role of protector by reducing the solubility of mineral composites in the organism. Another silica scientist, Leriche,[56] discovered that silica would intervene in a general way in oxidation and enzymatic phenomena. The decline in silica in neoplastic tissues would be in relation to the hormonal activity of the genital glands. This is why Monceau[57] prescribes the prophylactic addition of silica to sex hormone therapy used in cancer cases: it compensates for the weakening of the connective tissue.

According to Dr. P. G. Seeger,[58] silica should be added to basic cancer therapy as a defending and modifying element. Besides its beneficial action on cancer, lack of silica obviously contributes directly to increased risk of cancer, as can be gleaned from the Dunmaris well and the research listed. Beyond that, more in depth studies should be encouraged on the silica-cancer connection.

No Room for Rheumatism

Even more than its diuretic action, the beneficial action of silica on the connective tissues explains the usefulness of silica in the treatment of rheumatism. Moreover, the role of silica in the elimination of waste such as urea, uric acid and nicotine, reinforces the use of this natural medicine. Colloidal silica is, in fact, a catalyst of oxidation in the transformation of uric acid into more soluble urea. Therapy based on colloidal silica showed an increase in elimination of urea, uric acid and nicotine during an experiment which improved a chronic sciatic condition within five days.

Silica improves the elasticity of the joints. Dr. Charnot, head of research in Morocco,[59] discovered that silica always disappears from bones that are becoming decalcified before serious calcium loss takes place, as in osteoporosis. Dr. Charnot, using Kervran's aqueous extract of vegetal silica, treated many elderly patients suffering from painful musculo-skeletal disorders for over a period of seven years. In three to six months he achieved a dramatic increase in mobility and marked decrease of pain. He also found that sclerotic areas tended to disappear, while decalcified areas started to recalcify. This remarkable calcium-regulating function of silica has been confirmed by other researchers.[60]

Avoiding or Alleviating Alzheimer's

Silicon in silica may prevent the body from absorbing aluminum and may flush out aluminum from the tissues.

Aluminum in the brain tissue has been linked with Alzheimer's disease.

The British medical journal, *Lancet*, in its July 1993 issue, reported that researchers at the Newcastle General Hospital and at other research facilities in Britain, tested the theory that silicon could react with aluminum in the human organism, thereby preventing absorption of aluminum.

Volunteers were first given aluminum dissolved in orange juice. Then their blood was tested for aluminum. A significant amount of aluminum was found. Six weeks later, the volunteers were given aluminum and dissolved sodium silicate, a substance containing silicon.

The researchers discovered that in the second challenge with aluminum no aluminum was detectable. They concluded that "since the chronic assimilation of aluminum in the brain may contribute to or accelerate the development of alzheimer-type neuro-degenerative changes, a long-term increase in the dietary intake of silicon could prove to be of therapeutic value."

Although the researchers did not say how those at risk of Alzheimer's disease should obtain silicon, the conclusions are obvious. Sodium silicate is a scientifically purified silicon compound that is free of traces of other elements. Such compounds are specifically prepared for research purposes. Sodium silicate is not intended, and is not recommended, as a supplement to human nutrition. Silica from silica-rich foods or supplementary silica derived from spring horsetail are the obvious choices.

The exciting possibility of altogether avoiding or at least alleviating Alzheimer's disease makes one wonder if there is an interactive or even transmutational connection here between aluminum, silica, potassium and phosphorus. You see, both phosphorus and potassium are needed by the brain tissue for the mental alertness lacking in Alzheimer's patients. Re-read "The Dance of the Elements," on pages 19 and 20. You'll see why I wonder.

9

Why I Supplement with Organic Vegetal Silica

Practicing Prevention

The body constantly metabolizes silicic acid. It also continuously eliminates silica through such natural processes as urination,* hair loss, and the trimming of nails. Together this amounts to between ten and forty mg daily.[61] Because the average adult body needs to maintain reserves of seven grams of silica, it must compensate for the loss suffered; the body must be supplied with a similar amount to the amount eliminated to maintain silica equilibrium.

With increasing age less silica is assimilated. Often we eat less than in our younger years, or do not eat the right foods. Our bodies require larger amounts of silica during the later years for effective prevention. Silica deficiency and ailments arising from lack of silica have a direct influence on the degenerative process. Supplementation helps retard this process. The consumption of refined products

---

* Urinary excretion amounts to 12mg/24 hours (Source: Sochibo)

such as white bread, and peeled vegetables and fruits may lead to insufficient silica in the diet. Furthermore, regions where soil and water have a high calcium content are generally poor in silica.

According to Professor Loeper, daily silica needs of humans are 20 to 30 mg.[62] Supplemental use of organic vegetal silica extracted from springtime horsetail ensures that an adequate amount of silica is continuously available to the body. With adequate intake, enough assimilation of this vital nutrient can be assured even when the body's ability to assimilate is impaired. Any excess silica not needed by the body is automatically eliminated through the blood stream, kidneys and intestines.

All of us need silica, no matter our age. It is as important to give the body dietary sources of silica early in life as it is during the aging process when silica levels in tissue usually drop off steeply. Silica has a direct influence on absorption of all minerals that the body requires to maintain that feeling of well-being. Silica adds to the quality of life, and improves stamina and appearance. It can add a feeling of security by assuring the body does not miss out, and gets all the healthful nutrients it requires. I take two to four organic flavonoid chelated tablets or capsules* daily as well as choosing silica-rich foods. For remineralization purposes, such as bone mending, four to eight times that amount should be ingested until silica therapy has proven successful. This is best done under the supervision of your physician.

Silica Banking
Investing in your body through mineral supplementation is very similar to managing your retirement savings.

---

* Organic vegetal silica in capsule form should indicate clearly on the label that the content is of pure aqueous extract.

Simply make sure sufficient "silica funds" are in your "bone bank," bearing "healthy interest."

The Good, the Bad and the Right Silica

Finding the right silica may be confusing at times. There are different products available – which one should you choose? Make sure that the vegetal silica you use is 100 percent pure aqueous extract. Be sure also that it is from spring horsetail *(Equisetum arvense)* and no other horsetail species. There is a big difference (see Chapter 4 – Of Tall Horsetail Extraction). Watch out for packaging: if not bulk-packed, vegetal silica should be in tablet form or packed into pure gelatin capsules. You don't want to eat unnecessary fillers. Supplementary vegetal silica should be from a pure organic source and in soluble form to guarantee easy assimilation.

The best vegetal silica available in the USA, and the only one that is truly the original Kervran silica formula, is fittingly called Original Silica. It comes in easy to take, carefully designed tablets that ease metabolic assimilation in the human body. Original Silica tablets are made to the highest manufacturing standards and incorporate all scientific facts known about silica and its effect on the human body.

The active raw material, the horsetail extract, or silica extract, is made from horsetail *(Equisetum arvense L.)* that is harvested at the right time of year to make the ratio of water-soluble to non-soluble silica components as large as possible. The extract is produced by using solely water as the extraction solvent. No organic solvents or chemicals are used in this process.

Only such a careful process can ensure that there are no artificial solvents or chemical rest products left in a vegetal silica supplement. Because the extract in Original Silica is produced by means of using only water in the extraction process, it is also completely water-soluble. To the discerning consumer this means that the silica components included in the extract are water-soluble and therefore almost 100 percent bioavailable and assimilable by the natural body metabolism.

Just for a moment picture sand, glass, quartz, and ceramics, which are typical examples of minerals and products in which silica is the main component. It seems almost contradictory that the silica compounds that are normally hardly or not at all soluble in water would be rendered easily accessible to the body. The secret, of course, lies in the recovery method.

Original Silica extract is recovered from the horsetail plant at the right time of year. It is extracted with water so that the silica components are bound to the bioflavonoids which are naturally occurring in horsetail. This type of binding is called "chelating." The word derives from the Greek for "crayfish or lobster claw." This apt description gives a fine illustration of what occurs on the molecular level during the extraction process. A flavonoid molecule has the inherent capability to "grasp" the silica molecule from different directions in a claw-like way and carry it out into the water solution. In this way the solubility of silica components and their bioavailability can be increased a thousand times.

Original Silica tablets are made under continuous and strictest quality control. The active ingredient, the horsetail extract, is tested against several standards. Of these the silica content and flavonoid content are the two most important. Also, only raw materials of the highest pharmaceutical quality are used in manufacturing, which is under constant control and standardization. Kervran's Original Silica assures that you will receive a safe and efficacious product. All scientific knowledge about silica components and their availability to the human body has been carefully considered and implemented.

10

Horsetail Cooking

The Galloping Gourmet

Many modern foods are so refined, they no longer contain their original healthful ingredients. We eat white bread and white rice, we remove the silica-rich skins from almost all our vegetables. Resultant shortages of vital minerals are to be expected. Again, we are what we eat.

The following table shows the silicic acid content of various (unprocessed!) foods rich in silica that I recommend for increased silica consumption:

Food (100g)	Silica Content (mg)	Food (100 g)	Silica Content (mg)
Oats	595.0	Horseradish	13.0
Millet	500.0	Lettuce	6.0-7.0
Barley	233.0	Strawberries	6.0
Potatoes	200.0	Carrots	5.0
Whole Wheat Grain	158.0	Celery	4.0
Jerusalem Artichoke	36.0	Spinach	4.0

Food (100g)	Silica Content (mg)	Food (100 g)	Silica Content (mg)
Red Beets	21.0	Currants	2.0-3.0
Corn	19.0	Beans	1.6
Asparagus	18.0	Kale	1.6
Rye	17.0	Pears	1.5
Sunflower	15.0	Apples	1.0
Parsley	13.0	Cherries	1.0

On the lighter side, the above table proves that folklore does not always have it right. Despite a popular cartoon's propaganda, spinach will not really give Popeye – The Sailor Man – the bulging muscles he suddenly sports to keep Brutus from stealing his girlfriend Olive: oats would! Popeye should take his cue from powerful horses; they love oats! Nor will "an apple a day keep the silica-deficiency away."

Seriously now, the above silica values show that a *nutri-physiologically* valuable diet, consisting of organic vegetable nutrients can be followed by the healthy individual if preference is given to oats, millet, barley and whole grains.

Horse Without Tail
On the other hand, with increasing demand for silica (therapy, prevention, fractures, broken bones, aging symptoms etc.) therapeutic supplementation may still be advantageous. Silica deficiency may exist if your diet consists of too many refined foods. Silica is abundant in the shell of brown rice, in leafy greens and bell peppers. When food is processed, silica is unfortunately removed. Fiber is usually the first to be cut or washed away, and along with the fiber, the silica. Stripping cereals and otherwise processing foods has seriously depleted their silica contents.

This massive loss of natural silica in the diet has been paralleled by an increase in degenerative diseases.

Sauerkraut, EFA and Other Good Advice

Eat fewer calories, avoid processed food, choose fibre-rich natural food, eat less total fat, eat less saturated (animal) fat. You may wish to find out more about the right kind of oils to use. I recommend reading the book *Fats and Oils – The Complete Guide to Fats and Oils in Health and Nutrition* by Udo Erasmus. This excellent reference work is available at health food stores or can be ordered from Alive Books. Read the chapter on fatty degeneration. You will find that consumed in moderation, butter fat is quite ok unless you have a dairy allergy condition, and is an exceptional animal fat because it is not a body fat.

Check your blood cholesterol level periodically. Avoid solid and hydrogenated vegetable shortenings, margarine,* coconut oil and palm oil. Of course, unhydrogenated natural coconut is a good food. Avoid commercially baked goods, non-dairy milk and cream substitutes. I don't mean soy, rice, or nut milk, but derivatives of hydrogenated oils like coffee whitener etc. Start using cold-pressed vegetable oils like fresh flaxseed or safflower oils for your salads and dishes.

Eating right is a key to controlling disease. Add home-made sauerkraut to your food list. It contains important health-promoting nutrients. Find out how to make it, or obtain it from a health food store. It must not contain vinegar! The ingredients in home-made sauerkraut are reported to inhibit the formation of cancer in another interesting Alive book entitled *How to Fight Cancer & Win.*

---

* Orthodox medicine is coming around six years later! My margarine warning predates 1987. A 1993 medical study, also reported in *Lancet*, confirms the cardiovascular dangers of margarine or any fat that has been hydrogenated.

In this work on silica, I can only touch on the other vital issues of proper nutrition. So, do yourself a favor, check the recommended reading list in the back for complete information.

Quenching Your Thirst

Drinking sufficient liquids is vitally important to your entire body. The human organism is made up mainly of water. It is only natural that we should constantly replenish the water that we continually lose through breathing, perspiration and urine. It is truly astounding that this logical conclusion is widely ignored.

My eldest brother drank so little that I noticed it already in childhood and youth. Not so long ago I heard that he needed an operation to remove large kidney stones from his urinary tract. Afterwards the doctors advised him to take in more liquids to avoid a recurrence. If you feel you don't drink enough water, start drinking today. Best is non-carbonated water from a clean spring. Liquids are a most excellent way to cleanse your body. My book *The Joy of Juice Fasting* gives drinking guidelines and offers tasty, mouth-watering recipes for the successful use of liquids in fasting, reducing and spring cleansing.

Leftovers

The complex research compiled for you in the preceding chapters can be an effective tool when wisely used for disease prevention and the alleviation of ailments and degenerative processes that have not been or cannot be addressed successfully by orthodox medicine alone. In its modern application, orthodox medicine is not essentially concerned with freely available nutrients as remedies or restoratives. It is only concerned with the conventional treatment of symptoms.

Eat silica-rich foods wisely and supplement as may be required. You will have made a giant leap forward on the road to well-being, health and longevity. Take the best possible care of your body – it is the only one you have! It is also the proud vehicle of your spirit here on earth and should be kept in good repair. Enjoy the right lifestyle and foods to guarantee you happiness and long life! Be health wise.

Endnotes

1. Javillier, M., *Les éléments chimiques et le monde vivant*, Trait de Biochimie Génerale, 1960.
2. Kervran, C. Louis, *Biological Transmutations*, Beekman Publishers Inc, Woodstock, N.Y., U.S.A., 1972.
3. Lavoisier, A, *The Law of Conservation of Matter*, Popular Science, Vol. 4, The Revolution of Chemistry, 1968.
4. Goy, J., CNRS Research Supervisor, Doctor of Science, *The Value of Plant Organic Silica as a Dietary Supplement*, Paris/France, 1988.
5. Rosenauer, Herbert, *What are Biological Transmutations (Kervran)*, Swan House Publishing, Binghamton, N.Y., 1972.
6. Abehsera, Michel, *Foreword to Biological Transmutations (Kervran)*, Swan House Publishing, Binghamton, N.Y., 1972.
7. Rosenauer, loc cit.
8. Sochibo, *Pharmacodynamics and Therapeutic Uses (Horsetail)*, Paris/France, 1988.
9. ibid.
10. ibid.
11. Sochibo, loc cit.
12. ibid.
13. ibid.
14. ibid.
15. ibid.
16. Sochibo, loc cit.
17. ibid.
18. ibid.
19. von Goethe, J.W., *Faust, Part I*, Reclam, Stuttgart/Germany, 1971, "Wir sind gewöhnt daß die Menschen verhöhnen was sie nicht verstehen."
20. Kervran, loc cit.

21. Einstein, Albert, *Einstein on Peace*, Avenel Books/N.Y., 1981.

22. *Synthesis/Equisetum Arvense L*, Sochibo, Velizy Villacoublay/France.

23. Sochibo, *Pharmacodynamics and Therapeutic Uses (Horsetail)*, Paris/France, 1988.

24. Ref. "Herbal Medicine", Beaconsfield Publishers, Beaconsfield Books, England, 1988.

25. Sochibo, loc cit.

26. ibid (Leclerc).

27. ibid.

28. Schneider, Johannes, *Silica – A Vital Element for Good Health*, Alive Books – Focus on Nutrition, Vancouver, B.C./Canada, 1988.

29. Sochibo, loc cit.

30. Kamen, Betty, *Bone Health: A New Direction?* Let's Live, June, 1988.

31. Let's Live loc cit.

32. Sochibo, loc cit.

33. Sochibo, loc cit.

34. Pearson, Durk and Shaw, Sandy, *Life Extenstion – A Practical Scientific Approach*, Warner Books Inc, N.Y./USA, 1983.

35. Sochibo, Report on research of Huchard and Breitenstein, *Horsetail and Diuretic Action*, Velizy Villacoublay/France, 1988.

36. Goy, J., CNRS Research Supervisor, Doctor of Science, Paris/France, 1988.

    Loeper, J., Professor, Consultant Physician, Paris Hospitals, Member of the Académie de Médecine, Experimental Medicine Laboratory, Saint-Antoine Teaching Hospital Centre, Paris/France, 1988.

    Loeper, J., *Recherches sur le silicium dans les tissus animaux*, Thése, Faculté des Sciences, Paris/France, 1965.

Loeper, J., Goy-Loeper J. and Fragny, M., *The physiological role of silicon and its antitheromatous action*, Nobel Symposium, Stockholm/Sweden, 1977.

Loeper, J., Goy-Loeper, J., Rozensztajn L., Fragny, M., *L'action antiathéromateuse du silicum*, Bulletin Acadcademique Nat. Médicine 163, No. 6. pp. 530-534, 1979.

37. Taupin, J., *Contribution à l'étude clinique d'une d'origine végétale*, Thèse, Paris/France, 1960.

38. Sochibo, V., *Horsetail and Arteriosclerosis, 1 Study of silica in human atherosclerosis*, Paris/France, 1988.

39. Though the silica used in the field study was not derived from horsetail, it is nevertheless so impressive and indicative of silica's healing powers, that I have decided to leave it in this book on vegetal silica. Full details are given in the companion volume *Silica – The Amazing Gel*. As pointed out in that work, and as confirmed by other research, silica supplementation, similar to other mineral and vitamin supplements, can be quite efficaciously combined from vegetal and mineral sources. They are not in competition though their marketing to the public may well be – and rightly so – competitive.

40. Sochibo, loc cit.

41. ibid.

42. ibid.

43. ibid.

44. ibid.

45. ibid.

46. ibid.

47. ibid.

48. Schneider, J., *Silica – A Vital Element for Good Health*, Focus on Nutrition, Alive, Vancouver,B.C./Canada, 1988.

49. Sochibo, loc cit.

50 ibid.

51. ibid.

52. ibid.
53. ibid.
54. Sochibo, loc cit.
55. ibid.
56. ibid.
57. ibid.
58. Leibold, G., Kieselsäure – Urquell des Lebens, V.G.L.,Verlag, Karlsruhe/Germany, 1984.
59. Sochibo, loc cit.
60. ibid.
61. ibid.
62. ibid.
63. Sochibo, loc cit.
64. Geere, Gillian, Microbiologist, J.R. Laboratories Inc., Burnaby, B.C. A government designated and certified dairy and food laboratory, 1991, (author).
65. Schneider, Dr. Ernst, Wissenschaftliche Abteilung, Salus Haus, Dr. Med, Otto Greither, 8200 Bruckmühl, Mangfall/Germany, 1991.

Bibliography

Edmeades, Baz. 1986. "Nature's Recalcifier." *alive – Canadian Journal of Health and Nutrition #71.*

Goy, J. Doctor of Science. *The Value of Plant Organic Silica.*

Kamen, Betty. Ph.D. 1988. "Bone Health; A New Direction?" *Let's Live Magazine.*

Kervran, Louis C. Translated by Michel Abehsera, 1972, *Biological Transmutations – A New Science Practiced by M.D.s, Chemists, Biologists, and Nutritionists.*

Kervran, C. L. Translated by Crosby Lockwood. 1980. *Biological Transmutations.* Beekman Publishers, New York.

Leibold, Gerhard. 1984. *Kieselsäure, Urquell des Lebens.* V.G.L.-Verlag, Karlsruhe/Germany.

Lester, Paul C. B.Sc., Ph.D. *Equisetum – Family of Equisetacians Silica Update.*

Loeper, J. M.D., Ph.D. Consultant Physician, Paris Hospitals, Member of the Académie de Médecine Experimental Medicine Lab, Paris. 1988, *As a Dietary Supplement.* Sochibo/France.

Mahieu, Gerard. Sochibo. April 29, 1988. *Silica Symposium.* - Velizy Villacoublay/France.

Schneider, Johannes M.D., 1988, *Silica – A Vital Element for Good Health*, Alive Books, Focus on Nutrition No. 10.

Sochibo. 1988. *Silica and Cancer.* Velizy Villacoublay/France.

Sochibo. 1988. *Pharmacodynamics and Therapeutic Uses (Horsetail).* Velizy Villacoublay/France.

Sochibo. 1988. *Silica From Horsetail.* Velizy Villacoublay/France.

Sochibo. 1988. *Pharmacodynamics and Therapeutic Uses (of silica).* Paris/France.

Index

A

A-priori-knowledge 9
Abrasive qualities 29
Abscesses 48
Absorption of minerals 75
Acid-alkaline equilibrium 17
Acne 48
Active growing phase 30
Adipocytes 48
Age-related problems 64
Aging 2-4, 37, 41, 43-44, 48, 53-54,
    59-60, 63, 65, 78, 84
Alkaloids 31
Alzheimer's 40, 55, 74-76
Animal collagen 45
Animals 22, 36, 39, 71-72
Anti-aging remedy 59
Anti-inflammatory agent 61
Anti-wrinkle cream 47
Antigens 62
Antioxidants 7, 62
Anuresis 32
Aorta 36, 57, 70
Aqueous extract 31, 65, 74, 78-79
Arteries 17, 70
Arthritis 17, 45, 49, 62-64
Ascorbic acid 61
Assimilation of phosphorus 18-19, 36
Asthenia 18
Atheroma 16, 36, 70
Atheroscleroses 68
Atherosclerosis 49, 68-70
Atomic age 10-12
Availability to the human body 81

B

Baldness 50
Bathing in fresh spring horsetail 60
Bed sores 48
Beta-carotene 60
Beta-sitosterol 30
Bile 19
Biocatalyst 48
Biochemistry 23

Biological Transmutation 9-15, 24-26
Bladder 32, 64
Bloodstream 17, 63
Bone ailments 22-23
Bone calcification 18-19, 21-22, 38
Bone calcium 1-2
Bone cancer 73
Bone composition 38
Bone formation growth and
    maintenance 38-41
Bone mending 78
Bones 1- 2, 16-23, 37-40, 45, 49,
    60, 64, 71, 74, 84
Bowels 64
Brain calcification 54
Brain cells 64
Brittle bones 1, 37
Broken bones 23, 38, 84
Bronchitis 68
Burns 48
Burping 41
Buzzing of the ears 68

C

Calcification 16-22, 38, 54
Calcitonin 38
Calcium absorption by the bones 22
Calcium atom 10
Calcium carbonate 12
Calcium fluoride 17
Calcium in balance 18
Calcium in the bloodstream 17
Calcium migration 19
Calcium-regulating function of silica 74
Calcium reserves in the bones 20
Calcium-silicon balance 16
Calcium supplementation 1, 17, 22,
    37-38, 40
Calluses 48
Cancer 37, 39, 61, 72-74, 85
Carbon monoxide poisoning 14
Caries 51
Catalyst 36, 48, 69, 74
Cavities 40, 51

95

Coeliac illness 39
Cellular-oxygenation exercises 59
Cellulitis 47
Centenarians 65
Chelates 31, 80
Chicken theory 19
Chickens 12-13, 36
Chromatography 31
Circulation 67
Circulatory problems 32
Cold-pressed oils 57, 63, 85
Collagen 21, 39, 44-46, 51, 54
Colloidal silica 6, 74
Complexion 44, 51
Connection between silica and
  calcium 22-23
Connective tissue 2, 36, 43-46, 48,
  68, 70, 73-74
Conservation of mass and energy 12
Conservation of matter 10, 23
Constipation 64
Copper 29
Corium 45
Coronary atherosclerosis 67
Coronary disease 57
Cosmic rays 62
Cough 68, 71
Cramps 40
Cross-linkage 44
Cystitis 32

D

Daily silica needs 78
Decoction 32, 60
Deficiency in vitamin C 21
Degenerative process 2, 36, 43,
  53-54, 70, 73, 77,86
Demineralization 16, 49, 71-72
Deodorizing qualities of silica 6,
  32, 48
Dermis 45
Devil's claw 63-64, 103
Diabetes 69
Diarrhea 64
Diurectic 32, 74
DNA 44, 62
Dragonflies 28

Dysfunction of the intestinal tract 39,
  64-65

E

Eczema 32, 48
Edema 32
Einstein 11-12, 25
Elastase inhibitor 69
Elasticity 7, 17, 21, 45, 48, 51, 68, 70, 74
Elastin 44, 70
Elastogenic function 48
Electrical conductivity of the heart 20
Elimination 59, 61, 74
Enamel 51
Entropy 24-25
Enzyme, silicatase 30
Epidermis 45
Equisetum arvense 27-28, 31, 79
Estrogen 39-40, 60
Estrogen/progesterone difficulty 40
Excessive radiation 47, 61-62
Exercise 49, 55, 57, 59, 63
Experiments with guinea pigs 21, 72

F

Fatty degeneration 85
Feldspar 12
Fertilizing role of silica 27
Fetal development 2, 40
Finger nails 19, 49-51, 64, 68, 77
Flavonoids 30-31, 80
Flint stones 5-7
Fluoride 17, 38
Foot bath 32
Fractures 32, 37-38, 40, 67, 84
Fragile nails 49
Free radicals 44, 61-62
Frostbite 48
Fumaric acid 30
Fusion 15, 22

G

Garlic 57
Gastric irritation 33
Gastrointestinal tract intolerance 39
Genes 49

Genital glands 73
Gerontologists 65
Ginkgo Biloba 55
Glucosaminoglycanes 44
Gout 32
Ground horsetail powder 32-33
Gum problems 51, 68-69

H

Hair care 50-51, 55-56, 68
Hair loss 50-51, 55, 77
Harpagophytum procumbens 64
Headaches 1, 14, 68
Heart attack 63
Heart disease 57
Heart 17, 20, 41, 57, 63, 70
Heat death 24-25
Helium 14
Hemorrhoids 64
Hemostatic qualities of horsetail 32
High blood pressure 20, 57, 68
Hormone replacement therapy 39
Horsetail fern 27-30, 32-33, 79-80
Horsetail tincture 32
Humpback 37
Hydrochloric acid 39
Hyper-calcification 19
Hypertension 68

I

Immune system 54, 61-63, 67
Inflammatory rheumatic disorders 67
Injuries 38, 48, 64, 68-69
Insect bites 48
Insomnia 68
Interferon 61
Internal cosmetic 43-45
International Symposium on
  Osteoporosis 38
Intestinal tract 64
Itching 48

K

Kidney stones 64, 86
Kidneys 38, 40, 59, 64, 78, 86

L

Larynx 68
Lavoisier 10
Lime 15, 20, 37
Limestone 12
Linseed oil 63
Liver or kidney problems 40
Lost height 40
Lower back pain 40, 64-65
Lungs 19, 58-59, 65, 68, 72
Lymphatic system 68
Lymphocytes 62

M

Magnesium 13, 15-17, 19-20, 36, 40,
  72-73
Male fertility 61
Manganese 29
Memory capacity 55, 64
Menopause 37, 39, 60
Mental acuity 20, 25, 54-55, 76
Metabolism of calcium 19, 21
Mica 12, 20
Mineral silica 6, 18, 30
Mucopolysaccharide 44
Muscle tone 41, 59, 64

N

Nails 19, 49-51, 64, 68, 77
Negentropy 24-25
Nervous disorders 18-20
Nervous system 41, 60
Neurological illnesses 20
Nicotine 73-74
Nitrogen 14
Nose 59, 68

O

Organic acid 30
Organic vegetal silica 7, 18, 22, 33,
  40, 46, 48, 50, 53-56, 58-60,
  62, 77
Osseous demineralization 16, 71
Osteomalacia 16
Osteoporosis 1-3, 21, 37-40, 49, 58,
  60, 74

Oxidation 73-74
Oxycarbonic intoxication 14
Oxygen and silicon 36
Oxygen 7, 14-15, 36, 61
Ozone layer 62

P

Paleozoic or "ancient life" era 28
Pancreas 69
Pasteurization 11
Pennsylvanian period 28
Petrified wood 6
Pharynx 68
Phenolic acid 30-31
Phlebitis 32
Phosphates 19
Phosphorus 18-19, 36, 40, 76
Phosphorus therapy 18
Plant metabolism 27
Poisoning 14, 32, 55
Polishing and scouring with horsetail 29, 33
Pollution 58-59, 62
Poor nutrition 38
Potassium and decalcification 20
Potassium 6, 15, 19-21, 29, 76
Powdered horsetail herb 32, 33
Pregnancy 22, 48
Premature aging 7, 44, 54-55, 60
Premenstrual-tension syndrome 39
Preventive therapy 3, 14, 17, 32, 36, 38, 40, 44, 46, 49-51, 57, 59-60, 63-64, 74
Principle of entropy 24-25
Pulmonary tuberculosis 16-17, 19, 32, 71-72

Q

Quartz 6, 12, 30, 33, 80

R

Rabbits 36, 70
Rachitis 16, 22
Radiation 46-47, 61-62
Radioactive elements 62
Radioactive transmutation 11

Radioactivity 10
Rashes 48
Rats 22, 36
Recalcification of the bones 17, 21
Recession of gums 51
Rejuvenating effect 53, 65
Rejuvenation 65, 97
Remineralization 40, 73, 78
Reptilian eggs 14
Rheumatism 17-18, 32, 64, 67, 74

S

Salt of silicic acid 46
Sauerkraut 85
Scalp 55-56
Sciatic condition 74
Scientific doubt 25, 27
Secret formula 43
Selenium 61
Semiconductor 5
Sense of smell 61
Sex drive 61
Sex hormone therapy 73
Shampoo 50-51, 55-56
Silica and childhood 22, 37, 41, 58
Silica at birth 41
Silica-cancer connection 72-74
Silica capsules 78-79
Silica-containing moisturizing creams 60
Silica crystals 6
Silica deficiency 41, 49, 64, 77, 84
Silica equilibrium 77
Silica gel 6, 18
Silica-rich foods 55, 57, 64, 75, 78, 81, 87
Silica salts 70
Silica tablets 78-80
Silica therapy 18, 32, 49-51, 67, 69, 74, 78, 84
Silicate orologosilicate 46
Silicates 5, 27, 33, 75
Siliceous stone 15
Silicic acid 7, 11, 46, 48, 70, 77, 83
Silicification 6
Silicon atoms 6, 10, 16
Silicon carbide 6

Silicon dioxide (SiO$_2$) 5
Silicon 3, 5-7, 10, 15-16, 36, 39, 57, 67, 74-75
Silicon Valley 6
Skin ailments 3, 46, 48
Skin 3, 19, 21, 32, 43-49, 51, 54, 59-60, 68-69
Skin tumors 48
Sodium-Potassium Bond 15
Sodium-potassium transmutation 15
Sodium 6, 15, 20, 75
Soft-shelled eggs 20
Softening of the bones 16
Spores 29
Spring horsetail 27, 60, 65, 75, 79
Sterols 30
Stomach 39, 64
Stress 38, 46, 55, 57, 60, 65
Stretch marks 47
Striae 48
Stroke 70
Sulphur 13

T

Tetany 17
Theory of relativity 11
Therapeutic properties of silica 11, 30
Therapeutic silica supplementation 18, 37, 40, 46-49, 51, 53, 57-59, 62-64, 70, 77-78, 84
Therapeutical efficacy 30
Thinning of the bones 38
Tinnitus 68
Titration 31
Tonsillitis 32
Tooth decay 1, 51
Trace elements 29, 36, 63
Transmutation of potassium 19
Tuberculosis 16-17, 19, 32, 71-72

U

Ulcers 48, 64
Undernourished skin 48
Unsaturated fats 63
Urea 73-74
Uric acid 59, 73-74

Urination 32, 77
Urine 38, 64, 86

V
Vertigo 68
Vitamin A 60-61
Vitamin C 21, 61
Vitamin E 61
Vulnerary 32

W
Walking 56, 63, 67
Warts 48, 72
Water extraction method 33, 79-80
White blood cell response 62
Women die from fractures 37
Wound healing 32, 48, 61-62
Wrinkles 3, 45-46, 60

X
X-rays 22, 62

Z
Zinc 29, 61

Useful Addresses

Alive Academy of Nutrition
7436 Fraser Park Drive, Burnaby, BC, V5J 5B9,
Canada Tel.: (604) 435-1919 Fax: (604) 435-4888

Flora Manufacturing & Distributing Ltd.
7400 Fraser Park Drive, Burnaby, BC, V5J 5B9,
Canada Tel.: (604) 436-6000 Fax : (604) 436-6060

Hälsoprodukter AB Box 145, S-570 22 Forserum,
Sweden Tel.: 0380-203 90 Fax : 0380-211 40

SISU Enterprises Ltd. 312-8495 Ontario Street,
Vancouver, BC, V5X 3E8, Canada
Tel.: (604) 322-6690 Fax : (604) 322-6790

Scandinavian Natural Health and Beauty Products Inc.
Formerly Ecomer, Inc. 13 North Seventh Street, Perkasie,
PA 18944 USA
Tel.: (215) 453-2505 Fax : (215) 453-2508

Sochibo S.A. 8, rue des Fräres-Caudron,
CP 18 78140 Velizy, Villacoublay, Cedex, France
Tel (3) 946 96 76 Telex 699019 F

About the Author

Klaus Kaufmann is mainly self-taught. Historical events of World War II and the turmoil following denied him the privilege of completing university. Yet his thirst for knowledge remained unquenchable. Klaus has been studying natural healing for many years. His interest in horsetail goes back to early boyhood days when at the age of eight he grew up on the edge of a large forest. His search for a more natural lifestyle took him all over the globe. Following a photo safari to Africa, he decided to live in Southern Africa for some years. There he obtained first hand knowledge of a healing flora such as the Fever Tree, the bark of which is chewed by the natives to prevent malaria, and devil's claw root that is used in arthritis therapy. After getting married in Namibia, he took his wife to the equatorial reaches, spending a year on a teaching permit in Kuala Lumpur, Malaysia.

At the age of ten, Klaus won a prize for an outstanding children's story he wrote. After that his interest in writing blossomed alongside his growing interest in all matters relating to health. Following the study of English Literature and Creative Writing at university, his professor appointed Klaus editor of *CONTACT*, a Canadian Writers Guild publication. Under his editorship, the publication expanded from a simple newsletter to a magazine. When Klaus left, the publication was popular in book shops and read at universities across Canada and in England. A live performance in Toronto, *Jazz and Poetry* selected Klaus's poetry for a public reading. Before being published, Klaus worked as editor and as a ghost writer.

His enormously popular bestseller *Silica – The Forgotten Nutrient*, now in its second edition, was quickly followed by *The Joy of Juice Fasting* that also made the bestseller list.

During 1991, Klaus became concerned with the problem of mercury toxicity and wrote *Eliminating Poison in Your Mouth*. His 1993 bestseller is the companion volume to the "forgotten nutrient," *Silica – The Amazing Gel*. Klaus is currently researching electromagnetic field therapy for a new work on health, soon to be published. Klaus and his wife Gabrielle live at Burnaby Mountain in British Columbia.

Books Published by Alive Books

Books by Klaus Kaufmann

Silica – The Amazing Gel – An essential mineral for radiant health, recovery and rejuvenation, Klaus Kaufmann, 1993, 159 pp, softcover US$9.95 CAN$12.95

The Joy of Juice Fasting – for Health & Cleansing & Weight Loss, Klaus Kaufmann, 1990, 114 pp, softcover US$10.95 CAN$12.95

Eliminating Poison in Your Mouth – Overcoming Mercury Amalgam Toxicity, Klaus Kaufmann, 1991, 44 pp, softcover US$6.95 CAN$8.00

Devil's Claw Root and Other Natural Remedies for Arthritis, Rachel Carston (Revised by Klaus Kaufmann), 1993, 90 pp, softcover US $9.95 CAN $11.95

Other Books

Fats and Oils – The Complete Guide to Fats and Oils in Health and Nutrition, Udo Erasmus, 1987, 363 pp, softcover US $17.50 CAN $17.95

Healing with Herbal Juices, Siegfried Gursche, 1993, 219 pp, softcover US $16.95 CAN $18.95

How to Fight Cancer and Win, William L. Fischer, 1988, 287 pp, CAN $8.95

Making Sauerkraut and Pickled Vegetables at Home, Annelies Schoeneck, 1988, 80 pp, CAN $8.95

Recommended Reading

Trace Elements, Hair Analysis and Nutrition, Richard A. Passwater, Ph.D. and Elmer M. Cranton, M.D., Keats Publishing, Inc., New Canaan, CT, 1983, 385 pp, softcover US$14.95 CAN$20.95

The Joy of Health – A Doctor's Guide to Nutrition and Alternative Medicine, Zoltan P. Rona, M.D., M.Sc., Hounslow Press, Willowdale, ON, 1991, 252 pp, softcover CAN $16.95

All of the titles listed can be purchased or ordered at your local health food store or specialty book store. If unavailable, copies may be ordered directly from Alive Books at PO Box 80055 Burnaby BC Canada V5H 3X1. Please add $4.00 postage and handling, plus 7% GST to your order.